# The Feminist and the Sex Offender

# The Feminist and the Sex Offender

*Confronting Harm, Ending State Violence*

Judith Levine and Erica R. Meiners

VERSO
London • New York

First published by Verso 2020


3 5 7 9 10 8 6 4 2

**Verso**
UK: 6 Meard Street, London W1F 0EG
US: 20 Jay Street, Suite 1010, Brooklyn, NY 11201
versobooks.com

Verso is the imprint of New Left Books

ISBN-13: 978-1-78873-340-3
ISBN-13: 978-1-78873-342-7 (UK EBK)
ISBN-13: 978-1-78873-341-0 (US EBK)

**British Library Cataloguing in Publication Data**
A catalogue record for this book is available
from the British Library

**Library of Congress Control Number**
2020932049

Typeset in Sabon LT by Hewer Text UK Ltd, Edinburgh
Printed and bound by CPI Group (UK), Ltd, Croydon CR0 4YY

# Contents

# Introduction

## One Problem, Two Faces: Sexual Harm and State Violence

At the January 2018 sentencing of USA Gymnastics doctor Larry Nassar for the sexual assaults of hundreds of girls in his care, Michigan circuit court judge Rosemarie Aquilina did two extraordinary things.

First, she gave the floor to more than 150 victims, who were as young as five when Nassar's abuse began. What the doctor did, visit after visit, was put his fingers into the girls' vaginas and "massage" them—a kind of physical therapy sometimes used to relieve painful intercourse or incontinence, but never to treat the problems that typically plague gymnasts. Most of the girls had remained silent for years, fearing they'd lose their hard-earned perches as elite athletes.

"When I told my mom that it hurt, she thought I was referring to the pain in my back, not the pain in my vagina from the excruciating hour of assault that just took place," one woman testified. Said another: "I remember laying there frozen stiff on the table . . . I felt so powerless to control what was happening."

The women spoke of humiliation, fear, and long-lasting trauma: "Now I get flashbacks when I see male hands, and it makes me feel scared and threatened. This fear changed the way I grew up and how I related to boys. I didn't want to hold hands or ever be close to my guy friends."[1] As they testified, Aquilina praised the women's strength and courage.

Then she turned to Nassar. "If the US Constitution didn't forbid cruel and unusual punishment," the judge said, "I might allow what he did to all of these beautiful souls—these young women in their childhood—I would allow someone or many people to do to him what he did to others." Imposing a 175-year sentence, she pronounced: "I just signed your death warrant."[2] That was the second extraordinary turn. Was Aquilina giving other people in prison the nod to rape Nassar? Or kill him?

The room burst into applause. The judge became an instant star of the #MeToo movement. Tweets called her a "badass" and a "class act"; adulation circulated through the media. A few critics suggested Aquilina had overstepped her role as a supposedly unbiased adjudicator of the law. Fewer still spoke up for addressing sexual violence in ways that do not rely on punishment, and that seek accountability and healing rather than revenge.

We—Erica and Judith—were also enraged at Nassar and gratified that this time, women seemed to have prevailed over the abusers, harassers, and rapists. When photos appeared in every newspaper of a handcuffed and scruffy Harvey Weinstein, Hollywood power broker and serial rapist brought down by the revelations of #MeToo, it was hard not to feel a sense of rightness, of payback.

And yet, payback also felt unsatisfying—indeed, wrong. Because we know where that retributive impulse, coupled with politically fomented, racially tinged fear of crime, has led: to the buildup of the US carceral state, which imprisons more of its population than any other nation in the world, including those with far higher murder rates. The United States incarcerates women at eight times the rate of China and more than twice that of Russia.[3]

We also know where vengeance and punishment do not lead: to the end of sexual and gender violence.

## Two Problems, Plus Feminism

The Larry Nassar story offers a glimpse into two huge, interlocking problems.

The first is sexual violence: gendered and sexual harm, including child sexual abuse, and harassment, assault, and rape of adults. On one hand, contrary to what most Americans believe, sexual assaults of both children and adults have steadily declined over the past quarter century, along with the whole of what the state identifies as "violent crime," which fell by 75 percent from 1993 to 2017.[4] Yet, as #MeToo and cases like Nassar's dramatically reveal, harassment at work and on the street, "rapey" behavior on dates, assault by acquaintances and strangers, and sexual exploitation in schools, sports, and religious institutions are persistent and pervasive. They are "ordinary" occurrences, so seemingly inevitable and ineradicable that even as #MeToo (the phrase coined by activist Tarana Burke) began to break the silence, thousands of women and girls continued simply to shut up and endure.

### The #MeToo Challenge

This moment challenges those committed to transforming our carceral system—including people, like us, who are committed to justice for survivors of sexual assault and who also believe that prisons are the wrong answer to violence and should be abolished. We decry the system and advocate for change that is long overdue. Yet when that system ensnares people we loathe, we may feel a sense of satisfaction. When we see defendants as symbols of what we most fear, and that which we most greatly despise, we are confronted with a true test of our belief that no justice can be done under this system.

Kelly Hayes and Mariame Kaba
transformative justice activists
*The Appeal*, 2018[5]

The second problem is the state's "solution" to the first problem. That is, the sex offense legal regime, an ever-expanding body of laws and practices devised to punish and "manage" people with sex-related convictions: draconian prison sentences for a growing list of offenses; civil commitment (indefinite post-prison preventive detention in prison-like psychiatric institutions); and the sex offender registry, which is fortified by hundreds of local, state, and federal restrictions on where, when, and with whom registrants may live, work, play, travel, or just be. So radical is the marginalization of the large and varied category of persons labeled "sex offenders" that their existence has been called "social death"—a term sociologist Orlando Patterson used to describe slavery.

We call this a regime, but it is hardly a unitary or disciplined body of statute. Rather, it is self-contradictory and confusing, differing from town to town and state to state; many states do not fully comply with the federal laws, because it's cheaper to forgo the federal funds than to enforce the regulations. The regime does no good and much harm. It does not protect children or anyone else.

The laws' creators and partisans include elected officials in both parties; police, prosecutors, and judges; a sensationalist and credulous press; and public and private sector leaders, from school administrators to shopping mall managers to community activists—and feminists. Feminism is not to blame for the sex offense legal regime. But feminists—those who embrace what detractors call "carceral feminism," from the same root as the word *incarcerate*—have played a large role in sketching the blueprint and supplying the parts that make the machine function.

One kind of feminism helped get us into this mess. But a different kind of feminism is key to getting us out. The feminist, anti-racist, and anti-prison scholar and activist Angela Y. Davis used the term "abolition feminism" to signify a politics marrying struggles against interpersonal violence with those against the violence the state inflicts in addressing it—the ineffective, racist, and profoundly destructive prison industrial complex.

The abolition of the sex offense legal regime would improve millions of people's lives. People reentering the community after prison could find housing and jobs, repair old relationships and start new ones. If the police did not notify neighbors that these people were moving into the neighborhood, their children might not face bullying at school; their homes would not be vandalized. And almost twenty years of research concludes that eliminating the registry and community notification would not endanger children or the rest of the community.[6]

Yet even if the state eliminated this regime tomorrow, some other, equally egregious system would swiftly take its place, just as criminal justice "reforms" aimed at shutting prisons often simply mean finding cheaper, more technologically sophisticated ways to control people "in the community"—more ankle monitors, fewer jail cells and guards. Dismantling the institutions of policing and punishment is not enough. We must expose and resist the ideologies that make both the jails and the monitors "common sense"—and everything else a pipe dream.

Interpersonal violence and the violence inflicted by the state are not opposing actors in a moral or political war. Rather, the abuser or rapist and the criminal legal system are a team, the former the bad cop, the latter the good. They speak in unison: *Might makes right*. "If we want to get rid of patriarchy, we have to get rid of punishment," said the abolition feminist Mariame Kaba. The obverse is also true: getting rid of punishment would be a great blow to the power of the patriarchy, as well as that of white supremacy.

At its most radical, feminism is a challenge not just to the domination of women or of queer people. It is opposition to all forms of oppression. Feminism is also a vision of a world in which freedom from violence is not an end in itself, but rather the atmosphere in which all can flourish. That flourishing includes consensual sexual pleasure.

### *Problem 1: Sexual violence*

What do we know about sexual violence? A widely cited survey by the Centers for Disease Control and Prevention reports that nearly one in five women is the victim of attempted or completed rape ("including completed forced penetration, attempted forced penetration, or alcohol/drug facilitated completed penetration") in her lifetime.[7] Experts agree that most sexual and gender violence is not reported. In fact, almost 80 percent of sexual assaults are not reported to the police, according to a 2016 analysis by the Bureau of Justice Statistics,[8] as well as an estimated three-quarters of child sexual abuse.[9] Research also shows that women of color, poor women, people with disabilities, and queer, gender-nonconforming, and transgender people experience higher rates of sexual and gender violence than their cisgender, white counterparts.[10]

But statistics range widely, and they are affected by divergent criminal definitions, research methodology, and ideology. For instance, in 2014 campus anti-violence activists circulated the statistic that one in five female college students had been the victim of sexual assault. The Obama administration and much of the press adopted this statistic. Some quick journalistic work, however, uncovered that the number had been extrapolated from two flawed campus surveys completed in 2007. The researchers had counted incidents, such as having sex while intoxicated, that the respondents did not consider to be assault, and might even have been consensual.[11] A BJS analysis published shortly thereafter found that one in *forty-one* female students ages eighteen to twenty-four had experienced assault[12]—still an unacceptable number, if not the staggering one in five.

Why would researchers second-guess their subjects? Most obviously, such alarming numbers mobilize outrage and draw funding to a constituency or cause. But the campus rape researchers were not perpetrating simple dishonest manipulation. They were engaged in an ongoing feminist debate about how to name rape. One reason the surveyed women said they didn't report some incidents was that they didn't consider them serious enough. Well, said the study's feminist designers, they—and we—*should* take them seriously: call them sexual assault.

We can't just turn to the Justice Department or the FBI to clear things up, though. For one thing, there's evidence that police downgrade reported offenses—for instance, from assault to harassment—or discourage victims from filing complaints in order to artificially inflate their success in reducing crime.[13] And of course, sexual assault *by* police and prison guards routinely goes unreported, becoming an endemic "hidden crime," according to a study by Bowling Green University criminologists.[14] It's not just survivors who underreport.

Criminal statutory language, meant to be exact, is as ideological and obfuscating as any advocate's propaganda. For instance, the state makes a distinction between "forcible rape" and "statutory rape," the latter of which involves neither force nor threat—nor even, necessarily, an absence of consent, except in the sense that one of the partners is a legal minor (under eighteen in most states) and thus deemed unable to consent to sex. The message is that teenagers are not sexual and don't know what they want.

As far as we are concerned, if it is not consensual, it is rape. If all partners are able to consent, and do consent, it is not rape.

In the end, "crime" is a legal category and a volatile, malleable political term. "Harm," on the other hand, is a relationship and an experience. That's why we prefer "harm," which allows people to name and describe what happened to them. It also gives us room to talk about the ways in which institutions and the state hurt people, rather than just what individuals do to other individuals.

Moreover, simply counting the number of instances in which one person coercively uses the body of another person leaves the story of sexual violence largely untold. #MeToo brought down some powerful men. Yet powerful men continue to evade accountability, and, more important, the systems that shield them and naturalize their behavior go undisturbed. So do the interlocking oppressions of race, class, sexuality, gender, and ability that make some people the targets of harm at the hands of both individuals and the state. Violence suffuses our media and our politics; a disagreement can escalate to a death threat in the time it takes to type a tweet.

So feminists keep working to wipe out coercive sex. Meanwhile, two justices sit on the US Supreme Court who have been credibly accused of sexual harassment or attempted rape, and the man currently in the Oval Office is, by his own self-congratulatory admission, a serial sexual abuser. As we write, his twenty-second public accuser, the journalist E. Jean Carroll, has published an account of his raping her in a dressing room of the New York department store Bergdorf Goodman in the 1990s. When the story broke, it did not make the front pages of the major newspapers. The media that did cover it mostly repeated the president's stock response: "She's not my type"—not pretty enough to rape.

Most widely disseminated statistics fail to describe adequately the unequal distribution of sexual harm in our culture. Carroll, who is white, was wealthy enough to be shopping at the expensive store, and connected enough to travel in the same circles as Donald Trump. Yet, when asked why she didn't report the rape back then, she said she didn't think it would make any difference. As it turns out, she was right.

For women with little social or economic power—poor women, women of color, queer and trans women, sex workers, single mothers—this is not news. They often decline to report abuse or assault because they know they will not be regarded as credible witnesses, protected by the police (who in some cases are the perpetrators), or represented fairly by state agencies or in the courts. Having already suffered the criminalization of their communities, these women may not relish sending more men to prison. And they risk criminalization themselves: a woman who goes to the authorities to report being harmed by an intimate partner may find herself charged with neglect for failure to shield her children from witnessing violence.

### "Ain't I a Woman?"

Feminists and conservatives, gender theorists and genderqueers, white suffragists and Black abolitionists, Olympic judges and grammarians alike struggle over the definition of "woman." Our definition is broad and inclusive. As Sojourner Truth told us, anyone who identifies as a woman is a woman. When we talk about sexual or gender violence, we include sexual coercion of anyone targeted or vulnerable because of their actual or perceived gender or sexuality. Throughout the book we use "she" to refer to a survivor because the majority of people who experience gender and sexual violence identify as women. We use "he" to indicate the person who does sexual violence, because men perpetrate most of this kind of harm.

Or worse: women such as Joan Little, CeCe McDonald, Marissa Alexander, and Nan-Hui Jo—all low-income, nonwhite, and/or trans—have been imprisoned or targeted for deportation after they've defended themselves from life-threatening domestic abuse or gender violence.[15] The criminalization of women's survival extends to the arrest and incarceration of pregnant people who authorities deem to be endangering their fetuses because of drug addiction, depression, or self-induced abortion. This practice is now reaching unprecedented heights. In June 2019, shortly after the Alabama legislature passed the most restrictive abortion law in the country, Marshae Jones, a twenty-eight-year-old pregnant African American woman, was shot in the stomach during a dispute, resulting in the death of her fetus. She was charged with manslaughter for failure to protect the "unborn child." The shooter—instantly exonerated by "stand your ground" laws allowing a person to shoot to kill if she feels threatened—was not indicted. "The investigation showed that the only true victim in this was the unborn baby," said the police chief. While the charges were eventually dropped, the message was clear: not only was Jones illegitimate as a victim—not "innocent." Her body was merely a vessel. She was not even a person.[16]

### *Problem 2: The sex offense legal regime and the carceral state*

The experiences of CeCe McDonald, E. Jean Carroll, and Marshae Jones illustrate that some laws meant to protect women and children actually hurt them instead. This mismatch of intention (or stated intention) and consequences is not exceptional, however. It is a defining characteristic of the sex offense legal regime.

Feminists in the 1970s exposed the deep seam of child sexual abuse and sexual assault of women, hidden both inside the family and out. Out of these revelations emerged a powerful critique charging the patriarchal family—in which fathers make the rules and get what they want—as an incubator of violence against women and children. To give women the independence to take their kids and leave abusive men, feminists demanded such policy changes as equal pay, childcare, and affordable housing.

By the 1980s, however, with Ronald Reagan in the White House and conservative "family values" infiltrating government, the feminist critique was supplanted by its opposite. Now, the danger was the disintegration of the "traditional" white nuclear family. The culprits (in addition to those perennially indicted delinquents, Black single mothers) were white women, abandoning the home to enter the workplace. Not fathers and husbands, but depraved strangers—Satanist daycare teachers, child pornographers, and pedophiles—loomed as the monsters threatening "innocent" children. Suddenly, hundreds of daycare teachers—people working for low wages to enable mothers to go to work—were convicted of outlandish sexual depredations of toddlers: exposure to animal sacrifice, rape with forks and knives, abuse by evil clowns.[17] In 1994, carried on the wave of the sex panic, along with the racism-fueled crime panic that persisted from the Reagan years, Bill Clinton's Violent Crime Control and Law Enforcement Act passed with overwhelming bipartisan support.

Two sections of this "reform" bill laid the foundations of the current, overwhelmingly carceral—and increasingly overwrought—response to sexual violence. First, the Violence Against Women Act answered feminist demands for more law enforcement but ignored their pleas for more services for survivors, funding the former over the latter two to one. Second, under the Jacob Wetterling Act, states were required to set up sex offender registries.

The Wetterling Act was the first of the federal "child protective" statutes that would pile up like brick rows, each bearing the name of a white child victim of an extravagantly savage (and exceedingly rare) crime: abduction, torture, rape, and/or murder by a stranger. In 1996, Megan's Law mandated that states post the registries online and notify neighbors when certain registrants move into a community. The Adam Walsh Act, passed in 2006, expanded sex crimes statutes and penalties, established a public federal registry, and required that states publicly list "offenders" as young as fourteen years old. And in 2016, Barack Obama signed the International Megan's Law, mandating the placement of a "unique identifier" on the passports of anyone ever convicted of a sex offense against a minor.

While the sex criminal statutes stacked up, the state hacked away at the already-weak ramparts protecting children from the less spectacular perils of poverty—children who are disproportionately of color. As Clinton signed the 1994 crime bill, he also vowed to "end welfare as we know it." That meant capping cash assistance for parents and continuing Reagan's cuts to food stamps, public housing, health care, and education. The demolition of the feeble US welfare state was almost complete. And the attendant rise in family poverty has only made children more vulnerable to a host of harms—including sexual abuse.

The sex offense legal regime has continued to grow. Today, in many states and in the federal system, sentences for sex-related offenses exceed those for aggravated assault, arson, or even homicide. Some 6,400 people who have completed federal or state prison sentences have then been labeled "sexually violent predators" and indefinitely detained in civil commitment; most will spend decades inside locked psychiatric facilities, not for crimes they have committed, but for those they might commit in the future.[18] Some states have passed laws requiring chemical castration of people convicted of certain sex offenses.[19]

As of this writing, the number of names and photos on federal, state, and territorial sex offender registries approaches 900,000;[20] registrants' tenure generally ranges from ten to fifteen years, but for many (and in some states for everyone), it is lifelong.[21] And even if a person is removed from the official list, the Internet record is deathless. Advocates for the rights of registered citizens call the registry the "banishment list."

The requirements of the registry are stringent and copious. In addition to the usual conditions of parole or probation—mandated counseling, drug tests, curfew, and the like—registrants must check in regularly with law enforcement and inform them immediately of any new job, trip, car registration, or residence (even if the person is homeless). The requirements are interwoven with a web of restrictions. Depending on where he lives, a person with a sex-related offense may be prohibited from working as a retail clerk, fishing in a public park, volunteering at a polling place, putting up Halloween decorations, or (as recently happened in Tennessee) living with his own children. In some states, violation of conditions of sex offense parole or probation, no matter how minor, is a felony triggering additional prison terms as long as those for the underlying offense.[22]

People with sex-related convictions constitute one of the fastest-growing populations among the 2.3 million people locked in US prisons, jails, and detention facilities. The logic and technologies of the registries serve as a beta test for a vast "prison without walls," with electronic ankle bracelets, surveillance cameras, and tens of thousands of collateral consequences fencing in everyone convicted of a felony. Yet even relatively progressive reforms to the criminal legal system rarely touch "sex offenders."

### *Feminism: Part of the problem, key to the solution*

Rape and other interpersonal violence have been high on feminist agendas since the movement's birth in the nineteenth century. To feminists of all stripes, it is a patent and urgent fact that the threat and reality of sexual coercion rob all women, including queer and gender-nonconforming people, of bodily integrity and self-determination. And, as is true of abortion and other reproductive rights, without safety from violence, there can be no sexual freedom and no existential equality.

Yet feminists have never been unanimous on what to do about interpersonal violence. Should legal reform be the focus? And if so, what laws are the right ones? Can we change the culture to vanquish interpersonal violence? And if so, what changes will move us in that direction? Feminists have diverse answers to those questions, as we shall see. But for now, suffice it to say that by the twenty-first century, anti-violence feminists could be roughly divided into two factions: those who want to put abusers and rapists in prison, and those who want to abolish prisons and find nonpunitive, nonviolent responses to harm.

Both groups want to end sexual and gender violence. And both want individuals who do harm to be held accountable and those who have been harmed to be heard and helped to heal. But what does accountability look like, what is healing, and who is responsible for delivering these ends?

Carceral feminists—the ones who gave Judge Rosemarie Aquilina a standing ovation—are by far the larger and more visible constituency. These people equate accountability with retribution, a view shared by so great a majority of Americans that few would call themselves "carceral." Their ideas, they would insist, are simply common sense. That is why these feminists have been successful in realizing their priorities in major legislation like the Violence Against Women Act.

The other faction, far less visible or influential, arose in marginalized communities, among women—Black, brown, queer, trans, poor, disabled—whom the state has never protected. These abolition feminists have learned from experience that prisons do not end violence, but instead perpetrate and perpetuate it, while destroying individual lives, families, and communities. Like a lot of their compatriots in the carceral feminist movement, many are themselves survivors of sexual harm. But, unlike the other contingent, their politics join the struggle against sexual and gender violence with that against the "white supremacist prison nation," to use the term coined by abolitionist scholar Beth E. Richie.

In the effort to build alternatives to policing and incarceration, many abolitionist feminists are engaged in practices of restorative and transformative justice. Restorative justice, according to the New York Peace Institute, is "a response to harm that gathers all those affected by conflict to collectively decide how to repair the harm, reset relationships, restore trust, and rebuild a sense of community." Where the criminal legal system seeks retribution, RJ seeks repair; where players in the system may take only one "side" (either the perpetrator's or the victim's), RJ centers the needs of the harmed person yet never loses sight of the harm-doer's humanity, or the harm that may have befallen him.

Transformative justice goes further. In an interview in *Colorlines*, Mia Mingus, a San Francisco Bay Area educator and community organizer for disability justice, describes TJ as "a *political* framework" (emphasis ours) that asks, "'How do we respond to harm without creating more harm [and] without relying on state systems—the police, the criminal legal system, immigration and customs enforcement, prisons, the foster care system?'" At the same time, Mingus says, TJ works to "actively cultivate the things that we know prevent violence, things like safety, accountability, healing, justice, connection, and transparency."[23] When these practices are adopted by communities and constitute part of longer-term community-building efforts—and when they intentionally exclude the participation of any state actor or institution—they are sometimes called "community accountability."

## Solving the Problems: Fractured Resistance

"The people on the front lines against violence against women should also be on the front line of abolitionist struggles," declared Angela Davis in a 2014 speech. And those "opposed to police crimes should be opposed to domestic—privatized—violence."[24]

Feminist and anti-carceral movements must squarely confront the sex offense legal regime because it embodies some of the criminal legal system's cruelest practices. But there are other, less obvious reasons as well. For instance, the registry is designed to produce shame, and shame feeds a culture of sexual and gender violence and inhibits its survivors from speaking up.

Unfortunately, only rarely do people working in abolitionist and feminist struggles connect with those working against the sex offense legal regime. Focused in their daily practice on their "own" issues, these folks do not always cooperate, much less collaborate, with one another. People in the broad prison-industrial-complex abolitionist movement often marginalize or even openly denigrate those convicted of sex crimes. So do majority-white progressive movements; Occupy Boston, for instance, was riven by proposals to ban people on the registry from the encampment. None of this is particularly surprising. After all, social justice activists' anxieties about sex are no less acute than anyone else's.

For their part, the small network of "sex offenders" and their families working for the rights of "registered citizens" and those of the incarcerated or civilly committed for sex offenses do not generally have a robust critique of the prison nation. We often hear a mother say: "There are some people who should be in prison / civil commitment / on the registry—the *worst of the worst*. But my son is not one of them." On their websites, registrants' rights activists always stress the importance of preventing sexual harm, but too often they minimize the pain of those, particularly women and girls, who have been harmed.

These two movements also stand, for the most part, on two sides of a racial divide. Activists against the prison industrial complex are more likely to be nonwhite, while those advocating for men on the registry are mostly white. Moreover, neither has broadly embraced feminism. For many on the registry, feminism is public enemy number one. More than a few in the movement to abolish the prison-industrial complex—men, but also women—simply disregard feminism, considering it irrelevant to their struggle.

And no major resistance movement foregrounds pleasure and everyday happiness as primary progressive concerns.

Even to accomplish their own identified goals, these movements—feminism, registrants' rights, and prison abolition—need to understand each other's issues as akin to their own and find ways to come together in common struggles. Toward that end, one of our aims is to scrutinize some of the major conflicts between and among these movements and propose potential alliances. We neither contend that these conflicts are unjustified nor pretend that they can all be resolved. But opening lines of communication can help these now-separate movements find a shared analysis and build the solidarity without which none of us will win.

We can make a world that is safer, freer, and happier: one in which domination and violence are universally condemned and all can flourish. That may sound like a utopian, even deluded, statement. But, as every organizer knows, you can't plot a route unless you know where you want to arrive. This book concludes with a vision of that world—no compromises—and some ideas about how to create it. We contend that all these ideas are practical; in fact, most are already in the works. Organizing for social justice is not a matter of settling for one or the other—of dreaming of heaven or living on earth. What we have learned from the people whose brilliance is reflected in these pages is that a better world is not a destination, but a road. It is not a place, but a practice.

## Who We Are and How We Collaborated

We are feminist intellectuals and activists. Erica is an educator and a queer, Judith a journalist and a (straight) sex radical. We have both been "lucky" to experience only the "usual," "minor" sexual violations that come with growing up cisgender, female, and/or queer—homophobic slurs, gropes on the bus or on the job, dates that go scary. But like all women, our lives are shadowed

## Convo: Systems and Individuals

**Erica:** I'm worried that our work is operating at a very individual level—how individual people are treated. Yes, it is central to recognize this level of experience and analysis, but there's got to be a wider lens. We are part of movements, and we know that systems change comes from these collectives, not from individuals.

**Judith:** We are reflecting on movements, yes. But feminism is both individual and collective; "the personal is political" still means something. We keep talking about cultural change. Feminist cultural change happens both in the streets and in everyone's kitchens and bedrooms.

**Erica:** Yes, there's a blurring. But what we're missing is this commitment to seeing how these individual actions travel in a complicated landscape . . . actually, it is not that complicated.

**Judith:** Which is it? Complicated or not complicated?

**Erica:** Both! Take sexual violence: (some) men harm (some) women and usually get away with it. This is a familiar story and a seemingly uncomplicated one. The tricky piece is how institutions and their associated ecosystems represent and make meaning of this harm—some try to eliminate the harm, others trivialize or appropriate it for their political ends. And an added layer: white supremacist capitalist heteropatriarchy is always generating feelings that help maintain the inequitable status quo. We are all, in different ways, shaped to fear, "protect," and despise particular bodies. These feelings help do the work of oppression.

by the threat of worse. And this informs our view that the eradication of gender and sexual violence is a paramount task for feminism, and for all social and political movements.

Yet we also care about the rights and lives of people with convictions for sex crimes. As white women, we see ourselves in solidarity and struggle with the millions of people, disproportion-

**Judith**: To me, what's simpler is the systemic analysis. The complicated part is what happens inside people and personal relationships. Why do some men harm and some don't, even when they live inside the same systems? That's overdetermined, even mysterious. Plus, people make choices. If we get too far from the ground, we blame the system for everything.

**Erica**: What the movements I see myself as a part of aim to do is build rigorous and real pathways for people to be accountable and to transform and yes also to heal. Yet to end violence, we must build collective movements, not just practices and systems that operate at the individual level. And at the same time we also have to make more space for all the big feelings. People are angry, sad, scared.

**Judith**: The problem is how, right? And, where is that balance between individual feelings and the systemic analysis? My mother told me about a friend in her Communist Party cell who wanted to move to Florida because he had asthma and the doctor thought he'd do better in the warm weather. But the cell members were ready to expel him because Florida was a Jim Crow state and you weren't allowed to go there, much less live there. My mother told me that story many times; she said it was the moment she began to question Communism. Now, it's entirely possible that my mother was thinking more about her friend's pain than about the pain of people living under Jim Crow in Florida. But I also interpret that story as being about the cruelty of seeing systems more than people.

ately of color, who are monitored, disciplined, caged, and brutalized by the state. We do not accept injustice to some as justice to others. We believe that the sex offense legal regime must be abolished, along with the entire prison industrial complex.

In this book we speak in a single voice. That voice, like the statements of political campaigns and organizations, is the product of struggle; it expresses shared beliefs and understanding, as well as ways we've influenced each other and compromises each of us made for the sake of a cogent and strong argument. Still, we do not wish to appear as a monolith or put forth a party line. To let readers in on our differences, we've included snippets of taped conversations—"convos," like the one above—in which we articulate and work through some of those differences. We think they may be useful, as they also reflect conflicts that come up inside the social movements we discuss.

On a similar note, a word about the text: this book is a reconsideration and synthesis of much of what each of us has been thinking, doing, and writing for decades. So some of the text is similar, other parts identical, to work each of us has published before in articles and books of our own—and in a few cases, pieces we wrote together as Soros Justice Media fellows in 2015–16. These passages don't have quotes around them, as they're integrated into text original to this book, which, as our convos suggest, is a collaborative project in every sense.

# PART I

# Feminists Confront Sexual Harm

# 1

# Anti-violence Feminisms

In January 1971, New York Radical Feminists, a small group of white left-wing women, convened a "rape speak-out" at a church on Manhattan's Washington Square. Before a packed audience of 300, forty witnesses gave testimony. It may have been the first time American women gathered publicly to expose sexual violence without self-blame, shame, or apology.

One speaker recalled the grade school ritual of "depantsing," where boys chased girls to an empty lot, pulled down their underpants, spread their legs, and looked. Another woman had been raped by a gynecologist; a third was instructed by her psychiatrist to masturbate in front of him. Women told of rape by husbands and brothers, friends, comrades, and strangers.

New York Radical Feminists had decided to convene the speak-out when women started telling their painful stories in consciousness-raising groups. Now, in the sanctuary, women were publicly "speaking bitterness," as the Maoists used to call their collective ritual of class grievance. The writer Alix Kates Shulman later told Judith: "We were expressing *outrage*, the outness of rage."

Women had a lot to be bitter and enraged about. Police routinely ignored, ridiculed, or sometimes brutalized rape victims. Hospitals triaged them to the bottom of the queue, to be treated after the "real" emergencies. To be believed, a woman had to show the bruises of physical coercion and resistance, even though the rapist may have wielded a weapon or threatened to mutilate or kill her if she refused him. The prosecutor had to produce eyewitness testimony to a crime almost always committed out of sight. The defense attorney could bring up the victim's sexual history at trial to insinuate that she asked for it. In other words, a rape victim had to prove her own innocence before the rapist could be found guilty. Entire categories of sexual assault were invisible. No statute recognized marital rape; sex on demand was a husband's prerogative and a wife's duty. No one talked about child sexual abuse. There were few indictments, much less convictions, for sexual violence.

The organizers discouraged political rhetoric at the speak-out. But a few days later, they supplied their analysis in a one-page leaflet headlined "Manifesto of Shared Rape." Rape—like marriage and motherhood, control of women's labor and property, and domestic violence—was an instrument of patriarchal oppression, "final proof of [men's] power and [women's] debasement as a possession, a thing, a chunk of meat," the leaflet declared. "The act of rape is the logical expression of the essential relationship now existing between men and women. *It is a matter to be dealt with in feminist terms for female liberation*." Rape was not a matter of individual pathology but a central truss in the edifice of patriarchy, affecting all women, even if they were never assaulted. Rape was political, said these women, so the response to rape also had to be political.

Feminists organizing around sexual and domestic violence in the early 1970s demanded changes in police, hospital, and courtroom procedures, but few had much confidence in a state that had turned its back on women and children for so long. So within a few years, a network of feminist rape crisis centers and a parallel network of "battered women's" shelters sprang up across the country. Volunteers offered to accompany survivors to the emergency room or police station and through the courts, without pushing anyone to pursue any of those options. The women or their male friends provided security, not the police. Consciousness-raising sessions were held in the cozy, toy-strewn spaces. The goal was nothing less than transformative—in the words of the 1972 mission statement of the flagship DC Rape Crisis Center, "to abolish rape in our own lifetimes."

Throughout the sixties these women had seen Republicans—presidential candidate Barry Goldwater, California Governor Ronald Reagan, President Richard Nixon—promote "law and order," code for police crackdowns on communities of color, students, and protesters enraged by the murders of Black leaders and the slaughter in Vietnam. If white feminists' objections to this agenda came mostly from a political worldview, many women of color drew on personal experience. "Why bother going to the police?" asked Essie Green Williams, an anti-rape organizer with the National Black Feminist Organization, in an early 1970s interview. "The attitude of the police is that it's just another Black person who has been hitting on another Black person. You know, 'Ho-hum, they're at it again.' So Black women don't report rape."[1]

Legal reform was not entirely off the table. Liberal feminists like the National Organization for Women, dissatisfied with but not disaffected from the system, lobbied to repeal sexist laws, wrote model legislation, and met with police and members of the judiciary to educate them about women's frustrating and traumatizing experiences with the criminal legal system. Eventually, all these people, working both inside and outside the halls of power, won what are now considered basic survivor-supportive tenets of sex crimes law and courtroom procedure, such as the inadmissibility of an accuser's sexual history, the criminalization of spousal rape, gender-neutral definitions of sexual assault that include nonpenetrative and nonconsensual acts perpetrated on any sex by any other sex, and a system of court-mandated services for victims. By the 1980s, police precincts and district attorneys had special units to respond exclusively to sexual violence.

But anti-violence feminists from the left, especially women of color, were adamantly opposed to outsourcing vengeance to the state. "It must be made clear that rape is not a law-and-order issue," wrote New York Radical Feminists in 1974. "Women are not demanding castration nor are women demanding capital punishment. We do not want to make rape laws more punitive."[2]

## Carceral Feminism: Marrying the Violent State

By the 1980s, this militant, DIY anti-state spirit was moderating among the most visible, largely white, anti-violence feminists. The United States had begun to "govern through crime," as legal scholar Jonathan Simon puts it—that is, to address every social problem, essentially, by criminalizing it. Eventually, these women joined forces with tough-on-crime politicians and right-wing Christians determined to protect their conceptions of female chastity and childhood innocence.

Examining this alliance, in 2007 sociologist Elizabeth Bernstein coined the term "carceral feminism" to denote "the commitment of . . . feminist activists to a law and order agenda and . . . a drift from the welfare state to the carceral state as the enforcement apparatus for feminist goals."[3] Bernstein argues that carceral feminism is an expression of neoliberalism: a logic that blames social problems on individuals rather than on larger economic forces and systemic racial, gender, or geographic inequities and privatizes formerly public, tax-funded institutions and services, leading to their underfunding and deterioration. In fact, among the biggest predictors of interpersonal violence is male underemployment—a social, not a personal, deficit, and one that is exacerbated by neoliberal austerity. In the EU, austerity has also been linked to an increase in physical, emotional, and sexual violence against women. At the same time, budget cuts have decimated services for survivors and government programs on which poor women and their families rely.[4]

Leigh Goodmark, a lawyer for women who have suffered interpersonal violence, used to be onboard with the carceral crowd. "The antiviolence movement believed that if we made these problems illegal they would go away," she said in a speech at the International Restorative Justice Conference in 2018. But they didn't. The effect of arrest on recidivism, Goodmark noted, is "little to none,"[5] and incarceration may even make it worse. Legal discrimination against people with criminal records in almost every facet of life—housing, employment, and parenting—destabilizes both individuals and communities. For instance, thanks to poverty and broken social ties, almost 50,000 people each year leave prison and enter homeless shelters or end up on the streets (those with sex-related convictions are barred even from the shelters). And the criminalization of survival tactics and homelessness—arrests for shoplifting or sleeping on the street—land these people back in jail.[6]

## The Violence Against Women Act

The landmark achievement of the carceral anti-violence and victims' rights movements was the Violence Against Women Act of 1994. Finally, its proponents believed, the government would hold the perpetrators of intimate violence accountable. But perhaps VAWA's pernicious effects should have been anticipated. After all, it was part of Bill Clinton's bipartisan Violent Crime Control and Law Enforcement Act, which also created sixty new death penalty offenses, eliminated federal funds for in-prison college programs, poured billions into prison construction and police expansion, and required states to establish sex offender registries. At the same time Congress passed the crime bill, Clinton was also dismantling "welfare as we know it," as he put it. While the crime bill expanded and deepened the prison nation, VAWA married anti-violence feminists to the violent state.

VAWA nods to violence prevention, but it overwhelmingly leans on arrest and prosecution—in other words, criminalization, an option that fails to serve many women. Among the 1994 law's chief provisions were mandatory arrest in domestic violence situations—including dual arrests if the cops couldn't figure out who the aggressor was—and "no drop" prosecution, which prohibited the alleged victim from retracting charges. In some jurisdictions, the district attorney began to subpoena women to testify against their partners or jails them until they comply. By 2013, a Queens, New York, prosecutor told *Time* magazine that less than a quarter of victims cooperated.[7] Moreover, child protective services sometimes charge mothers with neglect or "failure to supervise" for allowing the children to witness their mother's abuse.

In 2005, the law was amended to "encourage or mandate arrest," and in 2018, to delete "mandate."[8] But the meaning of "encourage"—which remains in the statute—varies from precinct to precinct, and in fact may differ little from a mandate. In either case, the expectation of arrest has discouraged some women from reporting, since the arrest of either partner—or worse, of both—can lead to the loss of jobs, housing, government assistance, or child custody. To label one partner the perpetrator and the other the victim, furthermore, flattens the complexity of relationships that might be violent *and* loving, mutually destructive *and* positively interdependent. Therefore, to force legal action robs women of personal agency that is already compromised, and doing so steps up state control over them and their families. Leigh Goodmark describes the paternalism of this approach: "We infantilize people subjected to abuse because 'we care about you.' "

During its first twenty-plus years, VAWA may have helped a segment of certifiably "good" victims—that is, white, female, cisgender, middle-class, and educated ones. But it did not cleanse the system of its inequities, and arguably, it has worsened them. The criminal legal system views women of color, poor women, single mothers, sex workers, lesbians, transwomen, migrants, people in prison, and other Others with suspicion. Any of these women must prove her legitimacy as a victim—a quixotic effort. And VAWA has not only failed to help; it has hurt many people of color. For instance, by 2000, in Milwaukee County, Wisconsin, people of color comprised 24 percent of the population, but 66 percent of interpersonal violence defendants. Most of the cases were felony violations of criminal stay-away orders.[9]

While it was primarily feminists of color who had sounded the alarm about these state-perpetrated harms in the early 1990s, when VAWA came up for reauthorization in 2013, some of the white feminists who fought for it in those years also began to waver in their zeal. Karen Tronsgard-Scott, executive director of the Vermont Network Against Domestic and Sexual Violence, and a white lesbian from a working-class family, came to the work in 1995, the year after the law's enactment. "The law was all about building our relationship to the criminal legal system so it could do a good job. That had really good and really terrible consequences," she explains. The main terrible one: "A whole raft of survivors were left out, because the way that the funding drove the services was toward this relationship. In order to access the services, you had to have the prosecution."

The structure of VAWA, Tronsgard-Scott says, is upside-down: "Two-thirds of survivors want to have nothing to do with the criminal legal system, for lots of good reasons. But VAWA directs two-thirds of the funding to the criminal legal system and only one-third to victims services. That simultaneously forces the service sector into a container that moves further and further from a grassroots, community-based response and keeps them in a state of continuous scarcity." This scarcity of resources, she adds, also creates a poverty of vision and impedes work for social, economic, and racial justice. "There's just enough money to make things work, but not enough money to step back and ask: What are the root causes of violence, how are they related across oppressions, and how are we—the white women's movement—complicit in perpetuating those causes?"

## College Bound: Title IX

The carceral feminist logic that helped propel VAWA bled into other institutions, including colleges and universities. In 2011, under pressure from campus feminists who felt their colleges were not addressing sexual assault vigorously enough, the Department of Education Office for Civil Rights under President Obama issued a "Dear Colleague" letter to higher education administrations. The letter directed its recipients to set up procedures to investigate complaints of sexual misconduct and to discipline wrongdoers, or risk losing federal funds for violating Title IX, which guarantees gender equality in educational opportunity.

Almost as soon as the new procedures were in place, trouble ensued. The accused claimed they were being presumed guilty and denied basic due process. Other critics felt that university officers were not up to the job of investigation and judgment, and that the punishments at their disposal were too lenient; instead, they submitted, accusers should go to the police. Once the Title IX offices started ruling, lawsuits against the colleges piled up from disgruntled parties on both sides.

There was also evidence that this new criminal-educational hybrid enacted the racial and class biases of both systems. Consider, for instance, the assault accusations at Colgate University during the 2012–13 academic year, described by journalist Emily Yoffe in a 2017 article in the *Atlantic*. According to an Office of Civil Rights investigation, Black students comprised only 4.2 percent of the student body, but they accounted for half of the sexual violation accusations reported to the school, and 40 percent of the students put through the formal disciplinary process.[10]

In 2017, President Trump's secretary of education, Betsy DeVos, released amendments to the Obama directive. The policy changes added due process protections and, unlike the earlier iteration, allowed voluntary resolution without investigation. Groups representing the rights of the accused—some of them allied with the anti-feminist "men's rights" movement—welcomed the changes. But most anti-violence feminists denounced DeVos's move as a huge step backward, a tacit condonement of rape, and a betrayal of women who experience sexual violence.[11]

We think that the restorative and transformative processes are more compatible with the realities of sexual relations than the guilty-or-innocent criminal model, and more likely to achieve real accountability and change a harm-doer's attitudes and behavior. In fact, an increasing number of campuses, while legally stuck with the Title IX sexual misconduct regulations, are offering students this alternative. Still, there is little reason to believe a representative of the Trump administration wants to reduce racism or deal with sexual violence in a just and feminist way. The Obama letter was carceral in its logic; the DeVos amendments make a bad idea a little less bad (and aim mostly to undo all things Obama). The carceral state is the carceral state, whether surrounded by razor wire or covered in ivy.

## Outlawing Nastiness

In recent years, in online campaigns and law review articles, feminist lawyers and legal scholars have been pushing to ban a growing list of vile sexual behaviors. There's revenge porn, the nonconsensual dissemination of someone's nude or sexually explicit photograph or videotape; stealthing, the surreptitious removal of a condom during sex; and dating deception, or lying on dating sites like Tinder—something that, according to some research, 80 percent of users do.[12] Campaigners have called revenge porn "cyber-rape" and stealthing "rape-adjacent,"[13] and have claimed without evidence that they are ubiquitous and on the rise.

It's easy to see why somebody might like to outlaw these acts. They expose sexual partners to humiliation, fear, and anxiety, and to sexually transmitted infections and pregnancy. They are aggressive and misogynist. There are even online maggots' nests of unapologetic perpetrators—entomologically related to self-proclaimed "involuntary celibates," or "incels"—that promote such behaviors as the natural rights of men.

Some of these feminist lawyers, sensitive to the harms of criminalization, are careful to propose only civil penalties, or the establishment of these behaviors as torts—that is, harms for which a person can win damages in court. But the hyperbole—calling these acts rape—has roused lawmakers to criminalize them, and in some cases attach heavy penalties, including incarceration. In other countries, such laws have already been used to ugly, decidedly unprogressive ends. For instance, in 2008, Israel prosecuted the lover of a Jewish woman for rape, not because the sex was coerced but because the man had failed to clarify that he is Arab. In the UK in 2015, a complainant brought suit after belatedly "discovering" that a partner was trans.[14] And in dozens of countries, with the United States in the lead, conviction for HIV nondisclosure and transmission—a model for stealthing, and equally unprovable—has turned lovers into sex offenders.

## #MeToo

The impulse to criminalize a greater range of sex acts, from the merely obnoxious to the patently brutal, has found expression in some parts of the #MeToo movement. The revelations of widespread harassment have brought a range of responses, most notably the promotion and funding of more civil litigation. The Time's Up Legal Defense Fund, which has raised tens of millions of dollars to support lawsuits by survivors of sexual harassment and abuse at work, is an example of uncommon solidarity between high-profile celebrities and low-income workers.

Yet, rather than show the need for more expansive laws, #MeToo might be evidence that they are not the answer at all—that, absent thoroughgoing social change, the law does little to protect people from sexual harm. After all, the definitions and prohibitions of sexual harassment and the procedures for addressing it have been firmly established in US jurisprudence since the 1980s; they've been used, as they should be, to penalize thousands of workplaces that fail to protect employees from harassment or respond actively to complaints. But even successful litigation does not necessarily affect workplace cultures, whether on Wall Street or in Motor City, in a television studio or a tomato field. Ford Motor Company has paid out multimillion-dollar settlements over the last decade or more, but women workers say little has changed on the factory floor; they're still bringing lawsuits.[15] Often the workers most vulnerable to harassment, such as housecleaners or farmworkers, do not complain, because they can't afford to lose the job, or because they are undocumented and fear deportation.

In the end, there is a universe of ways that sexual partners can manipulate, hoodwink, and hurt each other. Civil litigation may offer some satisfaction—if the plaintiff can win, which is iffy in such cases. But a lawsuit is not politics. It may move money around, but it does not redistribute power. Only collective and systemic change, such as equal pay, affordable housing, strong unions, and free childcare, will enable women to demand sexual safety at work and leave bad relationships. And just as prison does not turn violent actors into peaceful people, litigation will not make a nasty person a considerate and honest lover. That requires the slow work of personal and cultural change, a transformation of social values so profound as to render unthinkable the misogynist acts that muscle out sexual mutuality.

# 2

# Intersectionality

Even among white feminists who cut their political teeth in the Black-led civil rights movement, anti-violence organizing in the 1970s and '80s remained largely racially segregated. Feminism spread organically through social circles, which rarely overlapped racial lines. Anti-violence workers were consumed with the daily crises of the women who came through the shelter doors; they did not stop to think about the racial makeup of their organizations. There were ideological reasons for this distance as well. Many white feminists hewed to the orthodoxy that women constituted a universal class, whose fundamental oppression supersedes differences of race, class, or sexuality. Rape is so profound and intimate a part of gender oppression, they reasoned, that organizing against it should unite all women. It did not.

In fact, that choice slowed cross-racial alliances against sexual violence for a long time. The early 1970s white activists' failure "to develop an analysis of rape that acknowledged the social conditions that foster sexual violence, as well as the centrality of racism in determining those social conditions, resulted in the initial reluctance of Black, Latina, and Native American women to involve themselves in that movement," wrote Angela Davis in 1990.[1] Other Black women cite different reasons. "Trying to deal with the rape issue when there are so many other issues of survival in the Black community—it becomes a matter of priorities," organizer Essie Green Williams said.[2] At the DC Rape Crisis Center, a Black client was more likely to be evicted than raped, noted the prominent African American women's health activist Loretta Ross, recalling the time she directed the center.

In their practice, some white organizations unintentionally reinforced the myth of the Black man as predator. In 1977, the all-white Dallas-based Kitty Genovese Women's Project culled the names of indicted rapists from fifteen years of courthouse records and published them. It was a bold direct action, and the group recognized they ran the risk of reinforcing institutional racism. "Such lists reflect a criminal-justice system which is much more likely to indict, try, and convict minority and low-income males than the affluent whites who may rape with impunity," they wrote. Yet they also wagered that their publication would "protect minority and low-income women who are doubly victimized, first by rapists and then by the courts, and that the list [would] be especially useful to them precisely because it contains a disproportionate number of poor and Third World men."[3] This was a presumptuous miscalculation, and feminists of color condemned the Women's Project for the very wrong it had feared committing: collaborating with Jim Crow "justice" by publishing a list of mostly Black and brown men in majority-white Dallas. These white feminists were again privileging sex over race, something their sisters of color could not and did not want to do.

## Intersections and Bridges

In 1977, the Black and brown feminist lesbians of the Combahee River Collective published a statement that reflected the misgivings and visions of many women of color in the sometimes-dissonant struggles toward gender equality, sexual liberation, and racial justice:

> We have a great deal of criticism and loathing for what men have been socialized to be in this society: what they support, how they act, and how they oppress. But we do not have the misguided notion that it is their maleness, per se—i.e., their biological maleness—that makes them what they are. As Black women we find any type of biological determinism a particularly dangerous and reactionary basis upon which to build a politic.

The collective rejected any analysis founded exclusively in the "sexual sources of women's oppression," because it "negates the facts of class and race." Lesbian separatism, a small but politically influential tendency in the white women's movement, was neither practical nor preferable, the collective wrote: "We struggle together with Black men against racism while we also struggle with Black men about sexism."[4]

Twelve years on, critical race theorist Kimberlé Crenshaw would popularize a term for what the collective was talking about. "Intersectionality" names the multiple identities and cultural, political, and economic conditions that make up a person and her situation. Intersectionality has profound ramifications for movement building, Crenshaw wrote:

> If any real efforts are to be made to free Black people of the constraints and conditions that characterize racial subordination, then theories and strategies purporting to reflect the Black community's needs must include an analysis of sexism and patriarchy. Similarly, feminism must include an analysis of race if it hopes to express the aspirations of nonwhite women. Neither Black liberationist politics nor feminist theory can ignore the intersectional experiences of those whom the movements claim as their respective constituents.[5]

At that time, there was a handful of forums where activists of color and their white counterparts in the anti-violence movement were confronting the white supremacy that damaged solidarity and efficacy. In a 1990 interview with Judith, Ross recalled fruitful conflicts over race at the DC center. At first, the clientele did not reflect the African American majority demographic of the city—because the center's staff did not. But the few workers of color enlightened their white colleagues about this, and the colleagues listened. The center amended its charter to mandate that the staff demographics match those of the client base. The center also recognized that the whiteness of its leadership would remain undiluted unless the center reached beyond the ranks of the feminist anti-violence movement as it was then constituted. So in 1976 the center hired Nkenge Touré, the defense captain of the Black Panther Party, to be its director; Ross, a housing activist, succeeded her. Both became “lifelong feminists,” said Ross, “but without that special effort, it wouldn’t have happened.”

Ross was a bridge builder in other ways, too. Despite resistance from comrades, she committed the DC Rape Crisis Center to the strategy the Combahee River Collective urged: to struggle with—not to the exclusion of—men around sexism. Responding to the requests of incarcerated men at the now-shuttered Lorton Reformatory, located just south of DC, Ross helped start a study group under the name Prisoners Against Rape. It was an early example of what might now be called feminist restorative justice: an alliance between feminist women and incarcerated men to understand sexual violence and work to repair the harm.

## Abolition Feminism

By the 2000s, women of color had begun to articulate another feature of the organizing landscape that was getting in the way of achieving true social transformation: on one hand, feminists addressing interpersonal violence were ignoring the violence of the state; on the other, anti-carceral movements were ignoring interpersonal violence. Women of color, disproportionately harmed by both, were left out in the cold. So in 2001, Andrea Ritchie, Alicia Beira, Mimi Kim, Andrea Smith, and others came together to form a national organization to address this mutual exclusion and work toward intersectional responses to sexual violence.

The result was INCITE! Women of Color Against Violence (now called INCITE! Women, Gender Non-Conforming, and Trans People of Color Against Violence), which the same year joined the national grassroots abolitionist group Critical Resistance in releasing a “Statement on Gender Violence and the Prison Industrial Complex.” Like the Combahee River Collective, these writers acknowledged the emotions of other feminists who had faced the same problems but turned to strategies with which they fervently disagreed. The INCITE!/Critical Resistance statement read:

> As abolitionists, we are confronted with the struggle between two conflicting forces for change . . . We share the feelings of outrage experienced by rape victims; we believe that repetitive rapists must be restrained from committing further acts of violence. On the other hand, we do not support the response of imprisonment. We challenge the basic assumptions that punishment, harsh sentences and retributive attitudes will serve to lessen victims' pain, reeducate rapists or genuinely protect society.

The statement called for "responses to gender violence that do not depend on a sexist, racist, classist, and homophobic criminal justice system." "To live violence-free lives," it said, "we must develop holistic strategies for addressing violence that speak to the intersection of all forms of oppression."[6]

A dozen years later, Angela Davis gave this political construction the name "abolition feminism." In a 2013 lecture at the University of Chicago, she began by speaking the names of Black women (including transwomen) victims of state violence and honoring the thinkers and organizers who came before her. Then she articulated this next phase of intersectional politics. "The people on the front lines against violence against women should also be on the front line of [prison] abolitionist struggles," Davis proclaimed. And those "opposed to police crimes should be opposed to domestic—privatized—violence."

# PART II

# State Violence: The Sex Offense Legal Regime

# 3

# Protecting (White) Innocence

On May 25, 1979, a blue-eyed six-year-old named Etan Patz left his family's loft in Manhattan's Soho, waved goodbye to his mother, turned the corner, and vanished forever.

In the next days and weeks, 500 police officers assigned to Etan's case interviewed hundreds of witnesses. When a four-detective team took over in July, they had more than a thousand reports on file. "We're following up every lead, every tip," Detective Thomas J. Finan told a reporter in July. The case was never declared cold. In 2012, when a new suspect emerged, cops excavated the cellar where the man said he'd taken the boy. In 2014, the FBI questioned a person in Europe as to whether he was Etan Patz, still alive. And in 2017, a fifty-six-year-old grocery store worker with severe mental disabilities, Pedro Hernandez, was indicted for Etan's kidnap and murder for the second time (the first trial, in 2015, ended in a hung jury). This time, going on no more than the defendant's inconsistent, nearly hallucinatory confession—and with another likely suspect in the wings—the jury convicted, and the worker was sentenced to twenty-five years to life.

"For Patz's long-suffering parents, Stan and Julie, it was the end of a bitter ordeal," *NBC Nightly News* reported when the verdict came down. Manhattan District Attorney Cyrus Vance Jr. suggested that it was not over just for the Patzes but for everybody. "We, as New Yorkers and as a community of families all over the United States, were . . . changed forever," Vance said in a statement. "Through this painful and utterly horrific real-life story, we came to realize how easily our children could disappear, ripped away from us right in our own neighborhoods."

Actually, it was, and is, anything but easy for such a thing to happen, especially in a neighborhood with nearly zero crime like Soho. Such crimes are vanishingly rare. According to FBI crime statistics, almost all missing kids turn out to be runaways and "throwaways"—minors whose parents would rather have them gone. If they're abducted, the culprit is usually the noncustodial divorced parent.

## "Other" Children

This is not to say that no American child was in danger in 1979, however, or that none is in danger now. The summer that Detective Finan, with the help of helicopters, bloodhounds, and psychics, was scouring Soho for clues to Etan's fate, other children were also going missing. In late July, the dead bodies of two young teenagers, Teddy Smith and Alfred Evans, were found in the woods of Atlanta, Georgia.

The *New York Times* reported Etan's disappearance within two days, and it would run 346 stories focused on or mentioning him before Hernandez was sentenced. Meanwhile, for four months the national press took no notice of the events in Atlanta; even the local mainstream papers were slow to report them. By October 1980, when out-of-town reporters picked up the story, fifteen children and adolescents were dead. By the time a suspect, Wayne Williams, was arrested in May 1981, the body count had risen to twenty-eight—twenty-two of whom were children and teens. The youngest, LaTonya Wilson, was seven, abducted from her home.

Unlike the New York cops, Atlanta police were not following up all the leads that came in over their hotline. As reporters from ABC's *20/20* discovered, they weren't even writing all of them down.[1]

What was the difference between Etan and these twenty-two Georgian children? He was white and middle-class. They were African American, from low-income families. To the media, apparently, Black lives did not matter, even the lives of elementary school children being taken in a slow-motion massacre. To the disappeared children's communities, it felt as if the elites running Atlanta, including its first African American mayor, were not terribly concerned about the poor.

For us, the amount of police coverage does not necessarily indicate city hall's concern for a community—particularly a community suffering from decades of disinvestment and probably too much, not too little, policing. Still, the allotment of resources to the investigation of murders says a lot about whose lives the state values.

"Still Missing": in white, middle-class society, the headline of the flyer featuring the silken-haired Etan Patz came to represent the loss of carefree childhood. The Patzes' tragedy was construed as a universal tragedy. The Atlanta child murders, once publicized, also elicited shock, grief, and anger. But their significance was assigned to a narrower constituency. This was not a public (i.e., white) problem. It was a Black people's problem; in some analyses, it was Atlanta's problem—unyielding racial division in a Southern city trying to market itself to investors as "too busy to hate."

In fact, Etan's abduction did not change "everything" for families across the United States, as Vance proclaimed. For white bourgeois families it changed nothing, except the perception that inspired them to adopt a hyper-vigilant style of parenting and lawmaking. Meanwhile, back in Atlanta and across the nation, poor Black children and their families continue to face myriad threats to their health and happiness.

A child, according to literary theorist Kathryn Stockton, is "a body said to need protections more than freedoms. And it is a creature who cannot consent to its sexual pleasure, or divorce its parents, or design its education—at least not by law."[2] But because race in America is the foundational arbiter of sexual innocence and guilt, only some children qualify as tenderly incompetent and deserving of protection, or even as children. Purity is white. The Child is pure, sexually innocent—that is, ignorant and desireless. So, sexually innocent children are white, and uniquely vulnerable to victimization. These vulnerable, victimized children deserve compassion and leniency, protection and nurturing.

In white American culture, nonwhite children are not really children; they're small (and potentially "bad") adults, in need of correction, not protection. A large body of research shows that authorities see Black children as more culpable of crimes— possessing adult intent and capacity—and thus more deserving of harsh punishment than their white peers. For instance, according to a study by the Georgetown Law Center on Poverty and Inequality, Black girls as young as five are seen as generally "less innocent," more knowledgeable about sex, and in need of "less protection and nurturing" than white girls of the same age.[3]

There is no LaTonya's Law, or any federal (or, as far as we know, state) law named after a nonwhite child victim of violence. Maybe that's because the violence that befalls children like LaTonya is considered unremarkable and unchangeable. Or maybe it's because policymakers understand that it *is* changeable—and their contribution has to be a massive investment of money to support Black, Native American, and brown children whose childhoods have been robbed by the "ordinary" conditions of white supremacy.

# 4

# Punishment and "Management": The Sex Offender Registry

What endangers children? How do we protect them? These, ostensibly, are the questions that launched a thousand sex offense laws.

Liberals in the 1960s, white and not, viewed family poverty as the greatest threat to child welfare, a linkage recognized by programs like Aid to Families with Dependent Children. Republicans (and a smattering of Democrats, notably Assistant Secretary of Labor Daniel Patrick Moynihan) blamed poor families—particularly Black single moms—for whatever harm befell their children. In the 1970s, new feminist theory (coming largely from white women) shifted the blame from mothers to fathers. The patriarchal family was a cauldron of spousal and child abuse, these feminists said. Their analysis stressed two pillars of oppression—sex and gender—but minimized others, notably racism and government power.

The necessary corrective to these partial (liberal or white feminist) or wrongheaded (conservative) notions came from women of color also avid to end interpersonal violence. The state, they said, abused and neglected poor Black, brown, and Native American children and their families, through neighborhood disinvestment, incarceration, and—in the name of child protection—revocations of child custody. They did not oppose public assistance in the forms of cash, food aid, or medical care, but, like poor people in the nineteenth century, they rejected the intrusions of "protective" bureaucracies that too often punished parents for being poor by removing their children to purportedly better homes. In the 1980s, the "family values" conservatives who put Ronald Reagan in the White House also wanted government to butt out of the family—that is, their authoritarian, heterosexual, two-parent, white Christian families.

There was no consensus as to what threatened children sexually and who was responsible for it. But there is one culprit toward whom social reformers, vice cops, victims' rights advocates, and sensationalist journalists have all pointed. He was called a white slaver in the nineteenth century, a sexual psychopath in the 1920s, a homosexual molester in the 1950s, a satanic abuser in the 1980s, and in the years since, a pedophile or child porn producer. The miscreant shape-shifted from era to era, but one thing remained the same: he was a stranger, lurking in the park, the church, the school locker room—anywhere and everywhere except the home.

By the mid-1980s, panic over "stranger danger" had spread like the Zika virus. After Etan's Patz's disappearance, the National Child Safety Council, borrowing an idea from a couple of Iowa dairies, launched a national campaign to print the faces of missing children on the sides of milk cartons. Etan's was the first. During its three-year duration, 5 billion of the cartons were distributed, but only one child, who saw her own face, was reunited with her father. She had been abducted not by a stranger, but by her mother and stepfather.[1]

As if to solidify the specter of the stranger-molester, in 1984 President Reagan created the National Center for Missing and Exploited Children (NCMEC) to serve as the nation's official source of information on child exploitation. This federally funded private agency circulates constant updates on the millions of hotline calls it receives about children assumed to be missing or abducted, and suspected child pornography and trafficking. The 2018 total: 18,462,421. NCMEC does not clarify how many of these tips are credible or substantiated. But we know this: very few. About 95 percent of minors reported missing have run away. Fewer than one-tenth of 1 percent were taken by strangers, and of these, almost all make it home safe and sound.[2] The writer Warwick Cairns calculated that, statistically speaking, a child would have to be left outside unattended for 500,000 years before being kidnapped by a stranger.[3] And if the odds of getting kidnapped are minuscule, the chance of getting killed by an abductor—not to mention kidnapped, raped, *and* killed—are so infinitesimal as to be statistically nonexistent.

### The Children's Corner

**1994. Jacob Wetterling Crimes Against Children and Sexually Violent Offender Act** requires states to set up sex offender registries.

**1996. Megan's Law** (amendment of the Wetterling Act) requires states to post their sex offender registries online and notify neighbors when certain registrants move into a community. The **Pam Lychner Sexual Offender Tracking and Identification Act** (named after the adult victim of an attempted rape who spent the rest of her life lobbying for the law) establishes a federal database.

**2005. Jessica's Law** (Florida, with other states following) significantly lengthens sentences and expands the registry's restrictions and surveillance.

**2006. Adam Walsh Child Protection and Safety Act** (reauthorized in 2016 without opposition) vastly expands sex crimes statutes and penalties, especially for child pornography and online offenses, as well as federal funding for enforcement. It establishes a federal registry and standardizes information in state and territorial registries on "offenders" as young as fourteen.

**2008. KIDS (Keeping the Internet Devoid of Sexual Predators) Act** requires jurisdictions to collect sex offenders' Internet identifiers in the registration process.

**2016. International Megan's Law** places a "unique identifier" on the passports of anyone who's ever been convicted in the United States of a sex crime involving a minor.

By the time NCMEC was established, research had already substantiated the early feminist theory about the perils of the patriarchal family: relatives and close family friends perpetrate more than 90 percent of child sexual abuse. Nevertheless, with the new agency providing cover, the government swung into gear building the sex offender registries and enacting their associated restrictions, whose goal is to protect children from predatory strangers.

Washington State created the first modern sex offender registry in 1990. State and federal laws followed, each named for the child victim of a spectacularly gruesome crime. More sexual acts, images, and fantasies were criminalized; new crimes—sexting, revenge porn—were codified. Nuisance infractions became misdemeanors, which became felonies. And every year, lawmakers craft new statutes from a seemingly inexhaustible store of ideas for policing sex and "sex offenders."

Thanks to ever-toughening sanctions, people convicted of sex crimes constitute "the fastest growing segment of state and federal prison populations," according to political scientist Marie Gottschalk. At the end of 2018, 12 percent of all people in state prisons were serving time for sex offenses; in some states the proportion was much higher. Of the nearly 180,000 people in federal prisons, almost 10 percent are in for sex offenses. The federal conviction is almost always for child pornography—the offense of production, accessing, or possession of sexualized images of minors.[4]

The recent anemic bipartisan efforts at criminal justice reform have had little impact on people with convictions for sex offenses. Almost all current reform initiatives exclude these individuals. In fact, even as policies soften somewhat regarding others who have broken the law, "sex offender" policies only continue to harden. Six months after Barack Obama became the first sitting president to visit a federal prison, he signed the International Megan's Law requiring that "Sex Offender" or another "unique marker" be applied to the passports of anyone ever convicted of a crime of a sexual nature against a minor.

## The "Banishment List"

Probably the single sex offense law with the greatest consequences was the federal Adam Walsh Child Protection and Safety Act of 2006, also known as the Sex Offender Registration and Notification

Act (SORNA). The law increased the number and scope of acts considered criminal and required states to create public Internet registries, placing people with sex-related convictions on them for a period ranging from ten years to life, or forfeit federal law enforcement funds.[5] As of 2019, NCMEC estimates the number of registrants at 900,000—a figure that serves both proponents of tougher restrictions, who use it to fan anxieties about the hordes of predators afoot, and opponents, who decry the number of their fellow citizens under Big Brother's watch.

Under SORNA, sex offenders must register in the jurisdictions where they live and report to the authorities regularly. State and local ordinances bar registered offenders from residing within a certain distance of schools, parks, bus stops, or other places children might congregate, often with the effect of banishing them from entire counties, or even whole states, as in Florida. On penalty of re-incarceration, registrants must immediately report any change in circumstances—buying a car, enrolling in school, or moving to a new address, even if the address is a street corner or abandoned warehouse.

Initially, federal guidelines required that each registrant provide local law enforcement with their name, address, photograph, and fingerprints. Today, many states take DNA samples, stamp "Sexual Predator" on driver's licenses, and/or mandate disclosure of logins and passwords to social media sites, if the registered individual is even allowed on the Internet. While federal law tells states to post photographs, physical description, date of birth, and information about the conviction on the Internet registry, some states also publish home addresses, and police may choose to notify the neighbors when a registrant is about to move into the community. These last two policies have led to vandalism of registrants' homes, harassment of their families, assaults, and even murder.

The restrictions increase not only in number and severity but also in absurdity. Many jurisdictions don't let registrants get a long-distance trucker's license, monitor elections at a polling place, shop in malls, or open their doors on Halloween. As the rolls lengthen, police departments can't keep up. Registrants tell us that they go to their local department and sit there all day, only to be sent home without reporting—which can be considered a violation of parole. Compliance with the terms of the registry does not correlate with a person's likelihood of committing another crime.[6]

### "Frightening" Statistics

Much sex offense statute and policy is rationalized by the claim that people convicted of sex offenses are highly likely to commit another sex crime. Research has firmly discredited this claim—it is in fact the opposite of the truth—yet it has proven almost indestructible, the perfect factoid upon which to fix unnamable fears. It first appeared in the legal record in *McKune v. Lile* (2002), a Supreme Court case upholding a Kansas sex offender restriction. Writing for the majority, Justice Anthony Kennedy reasoned that "untreated offenders" pose "a frightening and high risk of recidivism"—up to "80 percent." Recidivism is the state's calculation of the rate at which persons who have exited prison reoffend. In fact, the US Bureau of Justice Statistics calculates rearrest rates of sex offenders for new sex crimes at 3.5 to 4 percent.[12]

Where did the 80 percent figure come from? According to a much-cited 2015 article by Ira Mark Ellman and Tara Ellman, published by the University of Minnesota Law School, its origin was an unsubstantiated claim by a counselor writing in *Psychology Today* in 1986. The Ellmans found the words "frightening and high" in 91 judicial opinions, as well as briefs in 101 cases—legitimizing countless draconian restrictions and penalties.[13]

Make that 102 cases. Justice Samuel Alito repeated the phrase in *Packingham v North Carolina* (2017), an 8–0 ruling that a North Carolina law violated the First Amendment by banning registered sex offenders from accessing social media. The ruling was great news for registrants trying to survive in the twenty-first century. But it added one more citation for that damning phrase.[14]

Bills introducing new sex offender restrictions are surefire winners. "It appears that no proposed sex-offender registration law has ever failed a . . . floor vote in any state legislature," wrote Eli Lehrer, president of the libertarian think tank R Street Institute, in a 2016 *National Review* piece that was not entirely critical of the registries. "No state that has passed a sex-offender registration law has ever repealed it, and no law has ever been weakened in a substantial way."[7] The deputy director of the ACLU's Campaign for Smart Justice told *HuffPost* that he knew of no jurisdiction that had loosened its registry requirements without a court order.[8]

For the first two decades of the registries, such judicial orders were scarce to nonexistent. Court challenges came to naught; judges consistently found that the registries and their restrictions did not unconstitutionally deny due process, nor did they comprise double jeopardy (being punished twice for the same crime) or cruel and unusual punishment, because they were merely "administrative," not punitive, criminal measures. But as the registries have grown in size and the restrictions in extremity, this is beginning to change. For instance, in November 2018 US District Judge Richard P. Matsch concluded that Colorado's Sex Offender Registration Act had "effects that are analogous to the historical punishment of shaming and further resemble and threaten to result in effective banishment." He ruled that the registry and its restrictions violate the Eighth Amendment, which prohibits cruel and unusual punishment, and the Fourteenth, which guarantees due process under law. As of this writing, that ruling is on appeal.[9] But pressure is building. In 2019, the Colorado Supreme Court cited Matsch's opinion, among others, in ruling that the state's requirement of registration by people who committed sex-related offenses while juveniles was an unconstitutional violation of the Eighth Amendment. Writing for the majority, Judge Craig R. Welling suggested that his decision was part of a historical trend: he noted that other states were also reconsidering whether sex offender registration requirements are punitive.[10] Also in 2019, US District Court Judge W. Keith Watkins struck down the Internet-related restrictions in Alabama's

SORN law as violations of the First Amendment. "Sex offenders are not second-class citizens. The Constitution protects their liberty and dignity just as it protects everyone else's," he wrote.[11]

## Who Is on the Registry?

The fact that someone is on the registry doesn't tell you how dangerous he is, or even if he's dangerous at all. Registrants' convictions range from soliciting prostitution to rape, but it's hard to know what someone has actually done, because statutory definitions vary from state to state, prosecutorial "upcharging" and plea bargains predominate in criminal courts, and the language of a charge may not convey much about the harm committed or experienced.

Some things are known, though. Almost all registrants—93 percent—are male.[15] The overwhelming majority of their victims, according to the Bureau of Justice Statistics, are minors—as high as 90 percent, in states where the age of the victim is available.

The typical "sex offender" in the movies or on television is pasty and pale. And indeed, sex offenders comprise the only criminal population in which white people are represented roughly in proportion to their numbers in the general population: about two-thirds. While six in ten people in prison are nonwhite, about one-third of convicted sex offenders are.[16] Still, African Americans are overrepresented in the sex offense legal regime, making up 22 percent of publicly listed registrants nationally, but just 13 percent of the US population. Consistent with their treatment elsewhere in the US criminal legal system, African Americans are disproportionately charged, convicted, and sentenced, and compared with their white counterparts, they are subject to more punitive post-prison restrictions for sex crimes. Data suggest that the same racial patterns pertain to juvenile sex offenders.[17] Prosecutors are more likely to charge a man of color with rape, and juries are more likely to convict; African Americans are far more likely to be falsely accused and/or convicted of sexual assault than their white counterparts.[18] And the most-used risk assessment tool for sex offenders, the Static-99R, adds risk points for prior convictions for both sexual and nonsexual crimes, as well as charges that did not necessarily end in conviction[19] —all disadvantages for people of color, who are disproportionately arrested, charged, and convicted.

Interestingly, those who are closest to the action have grown less certain that these policies are rational, effective, or fair. We have spoken with unnumbered judges, lawyers, policymakers, parole officers, rape and sexual abuse counselors, and even prosecutors who agree that the sex offender registry is—we've heard this word a lot—a "nightmare." A few brave elected officials have spoken up. In February 2019, Michigan's attorney general filed a brief with the state supreme court arguing that the registry makes no distinctions as to the seriousness of individuals' offenses, that its restrictions are excessive, and that its tip line is conducive to public retribution and vigilante violence. The court may tell the legislature to rewrite the statute. But will the body support meaningful reform, or repeal? You might as well ask them to sponsor a bill to torture puppies every Friday afternoon on the statehouse steps.

SORN has created a permanent class of criminal pariahs. This is not just a result of the laws. We believe it is their intent. Bill Dobbs, an activist, press strategist, and curator of an online news feed covering sex-related law and policy, has a simpler name for the sex offender registry: the *banishment list*.

## A Fear and a Fantasy

Twenty-five years of experience and a mountain of research show that no part of SORN—not the registry, not community notification, not bans on candy distribution—gives the public any reason to feel either safer or less safe. In tracking the reoffense rate of a group of released sex offenders, the Minnesota Department of Corrections found that "not a single reoffense would have been prevented by an ordinance restricting where sex offenders could live."[20] A study comparing sexual offense arrest rates before and after New York State's Sex Offender Registration Act went into effect found "no support for the effectiveness of registration and community notification laws in reducing sexual offending by: (a) rapists, (b) child molesters, (c) sexual recidivists, or (d) first-time sex offenders."[21] Amanda Agan, an economist who studies SORN, summed up the data in an email: "The academic research has shown that registries and post-release notification laws do not on balance seem to be effective at reducing sex crimes or recidivism by sex offenders." She doesn't think the laws increase crime either. In other words, they have no effect on the incidence of crime.[22]

SORN is based on a fear and a fantasy. The fear is that the outside world is perilous, full of morally corrupting strangers. The fantasy is that the family is a sanctuary, where sexuality is limited to the monogamous relationship of husband and wife, and where the asexual innocence of children, including adolescents, is guarded.

But child protection cannot be based on irrational anxieties and saccharine dreams. Public registries and community notification are meant to enhance public safety. They do not. Nor do they help survivors reclaim their well-being. The only thing the registries accomplish is the registrant's social death. There is no reasonable defense for them. They should be abolished.

# 5

# Policing Deviance: What Is a "Sex Offender"?

Galen Baughman has been sitting in the Arlington County, Virginia, jail for more than three years on a technical violation of probation. The judge has denied bail. Baughman is prohibited from using the library or a computer, his reading material and phone conversations are monitored, and even therapy would not be confidential—"restrictions more typically imposed on a terrorism suspect," a group of supporters wrote to the Virginia attorney general. As of October 2019, Baughman has been in solitary confinement.

Also unusual for a man in his straits, Baughman is white, educated, and middle class, with a supportive mother and access to good lawyers and psychologists. When at nineteen a sex-related felony conviction, imprisonment, and registration ended his education and a budding career as an opera singer, Baughman turned to political activism and became an advocate for juveniles convicted of sex crimes.

Baughman is gay. He is now in his thirties and, possibly, still attracted to teenage boys. To those who write and enforce the laws, this makes him a dangerous criminal.

Baughman was convicted at nineteen for having sex with a younger teenage boy and sentenced to thirteen years in prison; he had also been arrested at fourteen for "teaching" an eight-year-old how to masturbate. Among the charges against Baughman was solicitation of child pornography, because he asked his fifteen-year-old friend to send naked pictures of himself. Baughman spent his twenties in prison, much of that time in solitary confinement. Upon his release, the state tried to civilly commit him—to lock him in a psychiatric facility as a "sexually violent predator." Legally, an SVP is someone defined as having a "mental abnormality" that predisposes him to commit another sex crime. It is a diagnosis concocted by Washington State lawmakers around 1990, and one rejected by the *Diagnostic and Statistical Manual*, the American Psychiatric Association's encyclopedia of mental disorders. Baughman beat the state that time. Over the last three years, although he has not changed in any relevant way, the state has been trying again.

This is how Baughman got in trouble: he attended a funeral in his hometown, with permission from his parole officer. There, he befriended a sixteen-year-old boy and began to text with him. The boy's mother found the texts and alerted the police. This, a technical violation of probation, and Baughman's first, would ordinarily merit a reprimand or temporary restrictions. Instead, the prosecutor took this long-distance epistolary relationship as evidence that Baughman, unable to control his deviant desires, was "grooming" the "victim" to accept sex. Even if he were "grooming," and even if he'd succeeded in recruiting this apparently straight boy into gay sex—a fear always lurking behind such prosecutions—Baughman could not be charged with statutory rape because the age of consent in the boy's state is sixteen. Still, the judge jailed Baughman, and the state began the process of trying to civilly commit him as a sexually violent predator.

The texts we have seen, which Baughman sent over a period of months, are both complimentary and self-aggrandizing. They may or may not indicate that he is attracted to teenage boys. Not children—he is not a pedophile—but youth, younger than himself. The boy's side of the conversation is nonchalant and terse. Even if he was impressed by Baughman's accomplishments, his texts do not show an innocent child in thrall to a nefarious sorcerer. Anyway, he lives hundreds of miles away. He could have ghosted Baughman at any time.

At the first hearing in this reprised civil commitment procedure, the psychologist Fred Berlin, founder of the Johns Hopkins Sexual Disorders Clinic, testified that Baughman is by no stretch a dangerous predator. Berlin did not question the demonization of the not-so-rare desire that is the basis of Baughman's criminal diagnosis: an adult man's attraction to a sixteen-year-old in fact, a common subtext of mainstream advertising.

Over the months of legal wrangling, the judge excluded all exculpatory evidence from the trial, including the testimony of two of its own appointed psychologists. Finally, in October 2019, a jury concluded that Baughman is a sexually violent predator. While the case is on appeal, he remains in jail. If the appeal fails, he could be locked up for life.

What is Galen Baughman's crime? He makes some people uncomfortable, disgusted. He does not fit the current definition of normal. But what is normal? "*Normal* is not an exact scientific term," Judith has written. "*Normal* is enormously susceptible to swinging with the gusts of politics and history. Disguised as scientific and fixed, it is subjective and protean."[1]

Among its fluctuations, "normal" can mean conventional or good or harmless or moral. And whereas "deviance" confers guilt, normality equals innocence. The category of normal and innocent—white, heterosexual, cisgender, sexually ignorant, desireless—is so narrow that even many children cannot squeeze into it. Teens have a harder time, and adults of any sex or gender can forget about it.

On the other hand, the category of deviance—*criminal* deviance—is extensive. The "sex offender" can be a man who exposes his flaccid penis to a woman in the park. He can be a man who climbs through that woman's bedroom window and holds a knife to her throat while he rapes her. The sex offender can be a habitual incest perpetrator, a teenage girl who texts a picture of her naked breasts to a lover, or a frail Alzheimer's patient locked in civil commitment.

The regime has many ways of policing the boundary between normality and deviance. As we'll see in the next chapter, one way is to declare someone mentally ill, then apply "treatment" that is inextricable, and sometimes barely distinguishable, from punishment. But there is still plenty of plain old-fashioned sex policing out there, and it is no surprise that the "deviants" policed with the most zeal are the same people regularly policed and caged by the criminal legal system at large.[2]

## "Underage"

Age confers relative levels of guilt and innocence. When two minors have consensual sex and one gets indicted for it, that person is almost always the older partner. Like other status crimes—acts that would be legal if an adult did them—sexual age of consent violations push young people into the carceral system. These laws suggest that psychological or developmental norms are static and natural. Looking at history and around the world, however, it is clear that they're not. For instance, as historian Holly Brewer recounts, in 1689 colonial Virginia nine-year-old Mary Hathaway married William Williams and two years later successfully appealed to the court for a divorce.[3] These two white people were considered capable, culpable, and competent. That was necessary, since life expectancy in the settler colony was twenty-five.

In the United States, age of consent ranges from sixteen to eighteen; a licit teen couple can cross state lines and instantly become criminals. Legal majority is lower in many developed countries: in France and much of eastern Europe and Asia, the age of sexual consent is fifteen; in Austria it is fourteen, and in South Korea, thirteen. The enforcement of the age of consent can reach the point of absurdity: a teenager who photographs herself and texts the picture to another teen can be designated both perpetrator and victim of the same crime.

In a heterosexual coupling, gender also plays a role in assessing who is the "perpetrator" and who is the "victim": the boy is more likely to be seen as the aggressor. At the same time, we can't quite decide whether girls should be protected from or punished for sex. So we do both at once. According to a recent report by the Coalition for Juvenile Justice, girls spend twice as long in juvenile detention as boys for status offenses.[4]

### When Feminists Fought to Lower the Age of Consent

As the age of consent has risen, most carceral feminists have been content to let the lines blur between the small, prepubescent people we used to call children and the fifteen- and sixteen-year-olds that much of the world regards as mature enough to make their own sexual decisions.

There was, however, a moment not so long ago when some decidedly un-radical feminists not only declined to support raising the age of consent but worked to lower it. In 1978, the New Jersey legislature was overhauling its sex crimes statutes. Anti-violence feminists and law enforcement pushed to toughen sexual assault laws, in part by raising the age of consent.

But other feminists, working with the National Organization for Women (NOW), foresaw a problem: they feared that prosecution of consensual sex between teens would divert attention from rape. To protect women and girls from unwanted sex without punishing girls for being sexual, they lobbied to lower the age of consent, from sixteen to thirteen.

In the end, pressure from a coalition of parents, priests, and police forced a compromise: the age of consent stayed at sixteen, but a "Romeo and Juliet" clause was added to exempt from prosecution opposite-sex sexual partners who were less than four years apart in age. This statutory corrective spread around the country in the 1990s, though not to every state.[5]

Like the Combahee River Collective, who saw that political demands focusing on gender violence alone, without attention to race or poverty, could harm marginalized women, the mostly white, suburban members of New Jersey NOW understood that without considering age, sex-related laws could backfire against the people they were meant to protect.

### *"Children with sexual behavior problems"*

In 1996, Judith wrote a piece for *Mother Jones* about a boy she called Tony, who was nine when he was charged with touching his eight-year-old sister's vagina and anus and "placing a pencil in her buttocks."[6] Once the charge was made, the child protective machinery began to turn; over three years, it nearly crushed the children and their mother. Fueling what a local psychologist later called the state's lethal combination of "zealotry and incompetence" was the determination that Tony fit into a newly minted class of sexual predator: "children who molest." Tony was cast out of the sheltered province of child sexual innocence. According to the local child protective agency, he was "a budding sex offender."

Toddlers as young as two were being labeled as children who molest and treated for "inappropriate" behaviors like putting objects inside genitals, pulling down their pants in public, or masturbating "compulsively." Some were being prosecuted as sex offenders. In fact, almost everything these children do—rub their bodies against other kids, expose themselves, insert things into orifices—can qualify as normative children's play. And even those children who do harm to others sexually almost always show signs of aggressiveness in other ways as well—hitting, abusing animals, setting fires. The problem is the aggression, the cruelty, or the inability to control their impulses—not the sex.

Nevertheless, Toni Cavanagh Johnson, the California psychologist who coined "children who molest" and wrote (off the top of her head) the first articles on the subject, was working from a deeply embedded, unproven tenet of American psychological ideology: that sex is a wholly exceptional—and, when gone awry, uniquely traumatic—category of behavior.[7]

Sensing that this new pathology was the invention of a sexually squeamish and/or profit-hungry crew, Judith dug around and discovered that, indeed, its inventors and popularizers were among the architects of the daycare and satanic abuse panics of the 1980s. This was another chapter in the sex panics, and part of the medicalization of sex woven into the ideology and workings of the sex offense legal regime.

## *Patient and perpetrator*

Twenty years later, at the 2016 convention of the Association for the Treatment of Sexual Abusers (ATSA)—held, incongruously, in a hotel next to Walt Disney World in Florida—a therapeutic subspecialty in treating children and youth with "sexual behavior problems" was firmly established. It would soon employ thousands of counselors and therapists in outpatient and residential facilities ranging from austere boot camps to programs described in almost cozy terms. A psychologist at one such residential treatment center, which takes patients as young as seven, referred to these children affectionately as "our little guys."

As in the adult sex offender world, the boundary between clinical and criminal—between "youth with sexual behavior problems" and "juvenile sex offender"—is porous, and a child can slip easily between categories. In one session at ATSA, a psychologist—one of three African Americans who was also one of a handful of men amid about forty, almost all white women—spoke of his distress over the criminalization of the boys he works with. Their families are Black and brown, burdened by poverty, unemployment, and substandard housing, he said. The teens have consensual sex for affection or pleasure. They get caught and are labeled as sex offenders.

"The kid says, 'I just thought [the sex] was okay.' The parents don't know it's not okay. They're being punished for not knowing something, and that punishment is going to have a direct effect for the rest of their life," the psychologist said. "Once they figure out they're going to be registered, they lose all hope of doing anything in their life. It is bleak."

Among minors identified as sex offenders, the age of contact with police peaks between twelve and fourteen. The vast majority of their presumed victims are younger children, according to the US Office of Juvenile Justice and Delinquency Prevention.[8] Yet the most comprehensive review of data on these youth—106 studies over seventy-five years, comprising 33,783 cases—also found the rate of committing another sex offense was below 3 percent.[9]

Is the United States producing an extraordinary number of

underage rapists who, once punished, straighten up? We do not think so. Rather, we attribute this statistic to several factors. First, the appalling lack of sex education. In 2016, fewer than four in ten US middle and high schools taught all the topics recommended by the Centers for Disease Control and Prevention as part of an "exemplary" sexual health education. The only topic that most schools cover is how to prevent the transmission of HIV and other STIs. According to the Guttmacher Institute, as of 2019 only nine states legally require students to receive information on contraception; in two, Utah and Tennessee, schools have to get permission from the Department of Education to talk about it. Twenty-five states mandate a stress on abstinence; five demand that any mention of homosexuality be negative. Only thirteen states require that sex educational materials be medically accurate.[10] If policymakers shrug at sexual ignorance—or legislate sex-negative disinformation—we know they're not educating students in negotiating considerate, mutual sexual pleasure.

But the most direct culprits for this alarming prevalence of juvenile "sex offenders" are the high age of consent—at eighteen, it is a year after about half of teens first have "sex," whatever that means—coupled with the widening range of normative child and teen sexual behavior that comes under scrutiny as wrong, sick, criminal, or all three. *I thought it was okay. I didn't know it was illegal.* If young people of average intelligence and moral judgment are breaking the law unawares, for acts even their parents don't know are illegal, then the law does not reflect a widely shared understanding of right and wrong, harmless and harmful.

## Queer

Now that gay and lesbian couples appear in the *New York Times* wedding pages, you'd think the bad old days of police raids on queer bars, entrapment, beatings, arrests, and imprisonment were over. But in many parts of the United States, for many people—trans, nonwhite, poor, homeless, or in prison, particularly—queerness is still a crime. Indeed, research illustrates an overrepresentation of queer people in the criminal legal system.[11] Even when laws are written neutrally, gender-nonconforming people and those engaging in consensual sexual activities with others of the same sex or gender are charged with a range of "quality of life" violations rarely brought against heterosexuals. One-fifth of trans folks surveyed by the National LGBTQ Task Force in 2011 reported being harassed by police, with much higher rates reported by people of color.[12] Lambda Legal's report *Protected and Served?* (2013) found high rates of police misconduct—unfounded searches, harassment, false accusations, and assault by police against trans and gender-nonconforming people.[13]

Analyzing the limited data from a 2011–12 US Bureau of Justice Statistics survey of people in US prisons and jails, researchers from the Williams Institute at UCLA Law found LGBT incarceration rates to be more than three times that of the general population—which is already astronomical at 612 individuals per 100,000.[14] The proportion of incarcerated women who are lesbian was 42.1 percent in prisons, and 35.7 percent in jails—a "shocking" prevalence, lead author Ilan Meyer told Reuters in 2017. "I had to check it three times to make sure we weren't making any mistakes."[15] That year, a Gallup poll found that 4.1 percent of US adults identified as LGBTQ.[16] Queer people are also penalized for consensual sex in prison: of the 1,118 respondents to a 2015 survey of incarcerated LGBTQ people in the US, more than one-third reported being disciplined for engaging in consensual sex. Of those, nearly two-thirds had been placed in solitary confinement as punishment.[17] The survey was conducted by Black and Pink, a national organization that advocates for currently and formerly incarcerated queer people.

Anecdotal evidence suggests a similar bias in civil commitment. For instance, there are enough gay and trans residents at Minnesota's Moose Lake facility that in June 2017 it held a month-long Gay Pride celebration, featuring transgender activist Ellen Krug as a special guest.[18] Patient privacy laws cloak information on civil commitment residents. But one way to crack into this information is to look at the criteria for who should be committed. On the ten-question checklist of the Static-99R (the chief risk assessment tool for sex offenders), more points are assigned to engaging in relations with another male, which increases the risk score—especially if that male is a minor.[19] The reason is that men with male victims have a higher recidivism rate, but this datum is confounded by the disproportionate rate of arrest and prosecution of men who have sex with men.

Queerness and age intersect to complicate legal prohibitions on consensual sex. Take for example, the case of Kaitlyn Hunt. In 2013, in Florida, the white honor student and cheerleader was charged with two counts of lewd and lascivious battery of a child. Hunt acknowledged having a consensual sexual relationship with a fourteen-year-old girl when she was seventeen. In Florida, the age of consent is sixteen. Charged just days after her eighteenth birthday, Hunt pled no contest to charges including battery and interference with child custody; she agreed to a deal that included four months in jail, house arrest for two years, and three years of probation, including the state's prerogative to monitor her electronic communications. Media coverage highlighted that the parents of Hunt's sexual partner were particularly disturbed by their daughter's queer sexual activity.[20]

## Too Old: "Elder Sexual Abuse"

The discovery of "elder sexual abuse," in the early 2000s, followed a predictable playbook. A well-meaning "expert" redefined consensual sex as coercion; a perpetrator was given a psychiatric-sounding name—the "gerontophile." This person was said to be driven by impulses far outside erotic and moral norms, yet rare as his tastes supposedly were, his numbers were said, inexplicably, to be mounting. Before you knew it, a panic was stirring.

In response to this newly discovered problem, several states banned registered sex offenders from working or living in facilities for the aged. Some nursing home professionals proposed facility-wide video surveillance. And lawmakers leapt to solve the problem the same way they approach children's sexuality: by eliminating the "victim's" legal ability to consent. In 2009, a thirty-eight-year-old Massachusetts state representative introduced a bill amending the state's child pornography law to add people over sixty to the list of those statutorily unable to consent to posing nude or performing sexually before a camera. The photographer, who could be a lover, artist, or spouse, would face a mandatory minimum of ten years in prison or $10,000 in fines if the image was created with "lascivious intent."[21]

Everyone has a right to bodily integrity. A person can be raped at any age, and sexual intrusion on the elderly is painful and wrong. But a far more common unhappiness for the old is the waning of consensual intimate touch. Furthermore, that right does not exist in a vacuum. The bodies of the institutionalized elderly are vulnerable to all sorts of insults, from overmedication meant to keep them docile to neglect of their pain. Queer people in nursing homes and senior citizens' communities experience ostracism or quiet nonrecognition of their histories and identities. Our culture infantilizes the elderly and is disgusted by their bodies. Worthy of praise are those rare institutions for the elderly that acknowledge and honor the sexuality of residents by protecting their privacy and enabling freedom.

## Intellectually Disabled and Neurodiverse

Nick Dubin was thirty-five in 2012 when an FBI SWAT team stormed his apartment in the early morning and arrested him for downloading child pornography. Diagnosed with Asperger's syndrome (AS), Nick had been flourishing—educated and employed, a competitive tennis player and an advocate for other people with autism. Now, with no prior criminal record, he faced a minimum prison sentence of eight to ten years if convicted.

Failure to read normative social cues, isolation, poverty, a history of rejection, and a dearth of sexual health information that addresses special needs: all these constrain the ways people with intellectual disabilities, and those who identify as neurodiverse,[22] can learn about sex and express their sexuality. Asperger's and autism are not associated with pedophilia or any other "paraphilia" (defined as a psychological disorder associated with abnormal sexual desires) yet people with intellectual or developmental disabilities are disproportionately charged with indecent exposure and other nonviolent public sexual behavior. "What gets AS young adults into legal trouble is not abnormal sexual desires, but their tendency to express or pursue normal interests in a manner outside social conventions," writes Mark Mahoney, a leading criminal attorney representing people with AS and autism.[23]

Nick's father marshaled expert evaluations attesting that his son posed no threat and that his disability required the court to acknowledge diminished culpability. As a white law professor with a white son, he got some traction: the sentence was reduced to five years' probation. Still, Nick is now a felon and a registered sex offender.

## HIV Positive

As of 2018, there were twenty-nine states in which a person can be prosecuted for having sex while HIV positive, and twenty-four of those states have pursued prosecutions.[24] The statutes call the offenses "nondisclosure" of HIV status and "transmission" of HIV; in addition to sexual acts, the latter can include sharing needles, donating organs, spitting or biting, or otherwise "exposing" others to bodily fluid while HIV positive. Some states enhance charges and sentences for other sex crimes, such as misdemeanors like prostitution, if the defendant is HIV positive; some impose decades-long prison sentences and require sex offender registration. These laws apply even if the sex is consensual and legal, the accused person wore a condom, or the complainant was not infected. The statutes can be ludicrous: in Arkansas, for instance, it is a misdemeanor to have your teeth cleaned without disclosing positive status.

The rationale for the criminalization of HIV transmission is that the virus is a deadly weapon. It is not. In fact, modern antiretroviral treatments allow people with HIV to enjoy healthy, long lives and also reduce their viral load to the point where transmission is virtually impossible; the prophylactic PrEP protects HIV-negative people from infection. By contrast, criminalization makes HIV more deadly. Such laws discourage people from getting tested, because they're only liable if they know their status, and from volunteering the names of former sex partners to clinics, for fear of being accused or prosecuted.[25]

## Harmed, not harming

Criminalization of HIV or of the sexual lives of people who are developmentally disabled exemplifies what geographer and abolitionist Ruth Wilson Gilmore has called "group-differentiated vulnerabilities" to policing, imprisonment, and premature death.[26] Analyzing racial and gender factors in HIV-specific convictions and sentencing in six states, sociologist Trevor Hoppe found that African American men received longer and harsher prison sentences. In three of the states Hoppe investigated, heterosexual men accused of not disclosing to women got prison sentences "roughly a year longer than their [gay] counterparts."[27] Although we are used to higher prosecutions of LGBTQ people, this discrepancy suggests that the criminal legal system values straight women's lives more than queer men's.

For their part, it is far more common for people with intellectual disabilities to be sexually preyed upon than predatory; they are seven times more likely to be victimized than the neurotypical, according to unpublished Bureau of Justice statistics. In the midst of the #MeToo movement, National Public Radio aired a series called *Abused and Betrayed*, about dozens of developmentally disabled women (and a few men) who had been sexually violated by institutional staff members, and whose cries were unheard, disbelieved—or, because of disability, unable to be voiced—often for years.[28]

In response to the series, several states took steps to legally protect the intellectually disabled from sexual violence. The legislatures did not, however, mandate training and good wages for caregivers or attendants of the disabled, most of whom are dedicated, kind, and paid execrable wages. And there was nothing in the bills about sex education for the disabled. Instead, California allocated extra money for prosecutions; Pennsylvania made it easier for such victims to testify in court; and Massachusetts proposed a registry of abusive caregivers.[29] In other words, the only responses were carceral.

Both of these categories of criminalization typify the management of risk in a neoliberal society. The HIV-specific laws create "an illusion of safety for those who do not have HIV or do not know their HIV status, putting the entire burden of HIV prevention on those who have been tested and know they have HIV," writes Sean Strub, executive director of Sero Project. "The statutes undercut the fundamental public health message that HIV prevention is a shared responsibility and that everyone should act in such a way as to maintain their own health and protect themselves from contracting HIV or other sexually transmitted infections."[30] And, we would add, to protect one another.

## Thought Crimes: Child Pornography

In a 2013 essay in *New York Times Magazine*, lawyer and journalist Emily Bazelon examined the laws that made it possible for Nicole (a pseudonym) to be financially compensated for videos and images of sexual abuse she suffered as a child. Her father, a former police officer, perpetrated and recorded the acts and distributed the images online, where they still circulate. In the years that followed, when other men were arrested for possession of child pornography and her pictures were identified, law enforcement notified Nicole, as required by a provision of a 2004 victim's rights law. The Violence Against Women Act also permits survivors of sex crimes to be compensated for the "full amount" of what they have lost. Nicole is still stalked on social media and called a "porn star."[31] She may indeed deserve restitution for her pain.

But any check she receives is a benign aspect of a secretive and rarely investigated function of the sex offense legal regime: child pornography law enforcement. In this area, criminal definitions have broadened, sentences have stretched, and convictions have mounted. Millions of dollars are spent on undercover sting operations "to catch a predator" that frequently border on entrapment.

The Supreme Court ruled in 1982 that the First Amendment did not protect depictions of minors involved in sexual activity.[32] The production of child pornography was criminalized—and for good reason: it involved forcing a child (then defined as a person under the age of twelve) into sexual performance. This is child abuse plain and simple.

At the time, such materials were rare—"as rare as the Dead Sea Scrolls," a New York City police official proclaimed in the early 1980s.[33] Today, thanks to the Internet, there are undoubtedly many more. But there is still no evidence that the consumer base is much larger, or that looking at such images transforms adult-attracted adults into pedophiles, or fantasizing pedophiles into active molesters—all of which are justifications for the massive apprehension efforts. To catch more potential predators, lawmakers have widened the net. Since the late 1980s, the age of a "child" in federal statute was raised first to sixteen and then eighteen. The child no longer has to be naked or doing anything sexual, or even a real person: computer-generated images are banned. In addition to the production of child pornography, state and federal laws have criminalized possession, receipt, distribution, or transport (which usually involve the same few keystrokes). They may include consensual sexting between minors. And along with these broadening definitions have come harsher penalties.

We in no way want to minimize the harm caused by having a picture of one's sexual abuse circulated all over the world forever. Still, the production of child porn—sexual abuse recorded on camera—is probably less widespread than the state wants us to believe. According to the BJS, of the nearly 20,000 cases of "commercial sexual exploitation of children" adjudicated from 2004 through 2013, fewer than 10 percent involved production.[34]

## Erotic innocence

Mystery magnifies the scariness of child pornography. It is a federal crime for any unauthorized civilian to access such material, even for journalistic or scholarly purposes. There are few trials—as in all felony indictments, almost everybody enters a plea deal—so juries rarely see the stuff. We are left to take the government's word on its awfulness and prevalence, and imagine the worst.

Anyway, the high-powered machine of child porn law enforcement would not have made Nicole safer. The cultures and institutions that enabled her father and shielded him for years remain in place. Sexual and gender violence is the problem, not fantasizing about children's bodies, as unsettling as many people find the latter. In fact, as legal scholar Amy Adler argues, these laws promote precisely what they seek to deter: sexual objectification of children. Child porn law sends the message that any gaze at a child's body is predation. Our anxieties about child sexuality, reified in statute, transform every adult into a voyeur and every child's body into a potential crime scene.[35]

# 6

# Medicalizing Violence

In a grubby clinic across from a trash-strewn lot on the edge of Dallas, about a dozen men and one woman sit in a circle of plastic chairs. The therapist who has invited Judith to observe asks the group if it is okay with them. Compelled to attend, with great incentive to please the therapist, they can hardly say no.

The session begins. Each participant reports on the week or reads from a completed assignment; the other members and the therapist, a white, middle-aged woman, comment. First up is James (not his real name), an African American man with dreadlocks, about twenty-five years old, who was a college football player when he was arrested for having sex with a high school girl he met at a game. He reads from folded-up pages he's filled in.

**James** (reading): *Outlets*: One-night stands. *Where and when did you start engaging in the behavior?* Freshman year of college, at nineteen. *How often?* At least two to three times a week.

**Therapist** (in a sympathetic tone): How many people? Thirty, fifty? More than a hundred? You have to have an estimate that's in a range.

**James:** Probably forty, forty-five.

**Therapist:** Write that down.

**James:** *What did you get out of this behavior?* Pleasure and self-satisfaction. *Why did you continue?* Because I enjoyed it. *Was this behavior a substitute for something else?* I put "no," but the group might come up with something else.

**Duane** (thirtyish, white, a senior member of the group): I'd say it was a substitute for a stable relationship.

**James:** You're probably right. I just thought it was the lifestyle of a football player.

**Therapist:** Did you feel you were part of a peer group? Did you get self-esteem?

**James:** Maybe.

**Duane:** Put "sexual gratification, peer acceptance."

**James:** The substitute was not to get close to anyone.

**Therapist:** Now we're getting close to it. You falsely assumed that sex equals intimacy. That felt pretty hollow, at the same time as feeling pressure from your peers. You saw women in general as having value only for what they could give you—money, sex, not as human beings or people with value all on their own. And now?

**James:** I definitely think different. [He pauses, waits for more comments, then goes back to the paper in his hand.] *Feelings after engaging in the behavior?* I felt good. I didn't have no remorse.

**Therapist:** Temporarily good, then shallow again? Then there was that loneliness, that neediness?

**James** (dutifully): It became an addiction, a cycle.

**Therapist:** So write that down.

**James:** Yes, ma'am.

This is "sex offender treatment" (SOT), a main element of the so-called containment approach to sex offender management, introduced in the late 1990s by Kim English, research director of the Colorado Division of Criminal Justice.[1] SOT is a condition of sex offender probation across the nation; in some jurisdictions, certain registrants are required to attend for the entire length of registration. Containment and SOT are based on the same assertion that justifies decades-long registration: that "sexual offending" is a unique, incurable psychiatric disorder that must be perpetually kept under control, lest it compel the person to harm again. In fact, there is no single profile of a "sex offender." And people with sex convictions have the *lowest* rate of recidivism of any "violent" criminal population.[2]

Containment is described as "victim centered": its priority is the safety and healing of the harmed person. In practice, this often means an aggressive disregard for the needs of the patient—the "offender"—most significantly, for the honesty, mutual trust, and confidentiality that most therapists believe are the prerequisites of a therapeutic relationship. But people with sex-related convictions are never taken at their word. They must admit guilt even if they are innocent, and cannot complete treatment if they do not (even though some psychologists have questioned the orthodoxy that admission of guilt is even necessary for successful treatment).[3] These clients are considered too sneaky to trust; "secrecy is the lifeblood of sexual offending," according to the Texas Council on Sex Offender Treatment. Therefore, "treatment providers cannot guarantee confidentiality."[4] Providers share whatever information they choose with parole officers, who also receive the results of regular polygraph tests.[5] Failure to make sufficient progress in treatment, as determined by the provider, can be a felony punishable by incarceration. In containment-speak, this hand-in-glove cooperation between the jailors and the putative healers is referred to as "multidisciplinary collaboration."[6]

## "Badness to Sickness"

The overlap of treatment and punishment in the sex offense legal regime is a part of a process critics refer to as medicalization. Medicalization is the reconception of differences or problems as medical or psychiatric disorders, often constructed as biologically caused, that need to be diagnosed, prevented, or treated. Often, marginalized sexual desires or acts considered immoral at a given time—homosexuality, pedophilia—are subject to medicalization, turning "badness to sickness," as sociologists Peter Conrad and Joseph Schneider write in their 1980 classic *Medicalization and Deviance*.[7] But the slippage is not just between nature and culture; it is also between the moral and the legal.

Asked how she defined sexual deviance, the therapist in Dallas replied, "Deviance is anything that's against the law."

## Feminists fight medicalization

Feminists have long been among the greatest critics of the medicalization of sexuality, as psychiatrists have sought to turn everything from clitoral orgasm to "frigidity" into a disorder, and to subject women to "cures" ranging from hydrotherapy to pink Viagra.

In the mid 1980s, anti-medicalization feminists staged a major, successful campaign against three new diagnoses proposed for inclusion in the American Psychiatric Association's third edition of the Diagnostic and Statistical Manual. One of these was "paraphilic rapism," described as arousal caused by committing sexual assault. Some researchers objected to this diagnosis because there was no evidence that rapists had the disorder and nonrapists didn't. Some feminists rejected the notion that rape is a mental illness, identifying it instead as a political and social institution. But it was the mainstream anti-rape movement, intent on putting more rapists behind bars, that spoke the loudest. A statement signed by the Committee on Women of the American Psychological Association and numerous other professional women's groups and individuals declared that the diagnosis would "provide an instant insanity plea for anyone charged with rape." These opponents submitted hundreds of comments to the revision committee and picketed the association's 1986 convention. "Paraphilic rapism" did not make it into the DSM.[8]

To this day, it is rare for an indicted rapist to be declared psychologically incompetent to stand trial or go to prison. But among the feminists who roared against the medicalization of sexual violence on the grounds that it might prevent a guilty rapist from going to prison, few have protested the use of junk science to legitimize indefinite preventive detention for crimes that might—or might not—someday be committed.

After the group session, the therapist announced she was retiring. The one woman in the circle began to cry. Indeed, while many registrants have recounted to us soul-crushing experiences of sex offender treatment, others report that they gained a lot from it. This makes sense. It is almost axiomatic that people who do serious sexual harm have suffered harm and trauma themselves. SOT might be their first opportunity to talk about their childhoods, express their feelings, or try to understand their behavior. We believe in psychotherapy.

But, contrary to the claims of the SOT industry, evidence does not support the effectiveness of sex-targeted treatment methodologies in reducing reoffense rates or improving clients' mental health. For instance, California's twenty-year Sex Offender Treatment and Evaluation Project compared three groups of people in prison with rape and child abuse convictions, some of whom got intensive treatment in prison and afterward, and some of whom got nothing. The study, published in 2005, found "no significant differences . . . among the three groups in their rates of sexual or violent reoffending over an eight-year follow-up period."[9] Therapist Phil Taylor, who used to be a licensed sex offender treatment provider and still works with men who abused, put it this way: "A lot of these guys might have been abused sexually or emotionally as children or are stuck in infantile perceptions of themselves." For their own well-being and other people's safety, he said, "they need therapy. What they don't need is 'sex-specific' treatment."

## Civil Commitment: Treatment without End

For those whose traits or acts once condemned them as willfully evil and now are deemed blamelessly ill, medicalization can be a good thing. If you cannot stop drinking, it's far more humane, and therapeutically fruitful, to be an "alcoholic" than to be a "lush." But in the medicalized world of criminology, a diagnosis can be as damning as a criminal conviction.

When illness is justification for punishment, the sicker the "sex offender," the longer will be his prison sentence and registration and the stricter its terms. And if the aim is even longer punishment, then an even more serious diagnosis is called for. So in 1990, in the heat of a panic following the abduction, rape, and murder of a young woman by a man with a sex conviction who was out on work release, some Washington State legislators cooked one up: a "sexually violent predator" (SVP) is a person who suffers from a "mental abnormality" predisposing him to commit sex crimes. The diagnosis, like the clinical designation "sex offender," is based on the fact that the person has committed sex crimes before. The state's Community Protection Act allowed it to lock up this person in psychiatric civil commitment indefinitely after the completion of a prison sentence, even if he'd been declared sane enough to stand trial and be convicted.

The APA condemned the SVP diagnosis in 1999 as "vague and circular" and a "misuse of psychiatry . . . to effect nonmedical societal"—that is, punitive—"ends."[10] Three scholars who reviewed the lobbying, drafting, and passage of Washington's SVP legislation concluded that civil commitment had no therapeutic or criminological basis. Looking at California data and other research on the negligible effect of sex offender treatment, they concluded: "It seems to follow that the explanation for the Community Protection Act is political."[11]

Nevertheless, following Washington's lead, nineteen other states and the federal government enacted SVP laws, creating a gulag of psychiatric prisons where detainees are invisible and forgotten by pretty much everyone but their loved ones. As of March 2019, there were 6,400 people in civil commitment, according to the Prison Policy Initiative; almost all are male.[12] Some are the storied "worst of the worst," like the man Washington's law was passed to contend with. Others are more like the immature teenager confined in Illinois for repeated indecent exposure when he was a minor, and for what he says was consensual sex with a fifteen-year-old when he was twenty. Some are in for child porn possession. Others remain in limbo, like Galen Baughman, sitting in a Virginia jail cell contemplating life in lockup while his lawyers appeal his conviction as an SVP.

People in civil commitment are called patients, but they live in prison-like settings, with prison-like practices—cell raids, lockdowns, solitary confinement, and censorship of what they may view, read, or listen to. Patients at Coalinga State Hospital in California refer to themselves as "hosprisoners." Treatment, the ostensible reason for which these people are locked up, is one of the main sources of their frustration and demoralization, some to the point of suicidal depression. Year after year they climb a downward escalator of repetitive sessions, almost reaching the top only to earn demotions for such Kafkaesque infractions as "treatment fatigue." Questioning the value of these exercises or protesting confinement is self-defeating, since an entry on the books of "resistance" or "defiance" is evidence that the complainer is not only crazy, but also refusing to get better.

### *Risky assessment*

Almost every "sexually violent predator" got that label based on the same "risk assessment tool": the Static-99R. This instrument assigns points for fixed, or "static," attributes, such as the age of the person and his victim, to produce an algorithm that purports to determine the odds of reoffense. The factor given the most weight is past convictions for both sexual and nonsexual offenses; this category also includes sex-related *charges*, whether or not they resulted in conviction.[13] Numerous analyses have found biases built into all criminal risk assessment tools, and the Static-99R is no different.[14] In these evaluations, sex-specific actuarial tools consistently show "moderate" accuracy in predicting recidivism; a recent meta-analysis found that the Static-99R gets it right about 60 percent of the time[15]—"not much better than a coin toss," one expert commented.[16] Even R. Karl Hanson, one of the Static-99R's authors, has published an analysis of statistical models of recidivism that casts doubt on his own creation, and on the wider assumption that a rap sheet is a predictive document. After ten years, the risk of reoffense for people with records of sexual or nonsexual offenses was about the same as for people with no criminal record. "People change," Hanson averred. "Desistance"—ceasing to commit crimes—"is the norm."[17]

## *No rights*

The Supreme Court ruled in 1997, in *Kansas v. Hendricks*, that civil commitment of people convicted of sex offenses is not criminal but administrative, not punitive but therapeutic. This meant that continued detention without additional conviction could not be rejected as unconstitutional double jeopardy (being punished twice for the same crime), or as cruel and unusual punishment.

Still, there has been progress. Armed with a twenty-year record of abuses and failures—as well as the evidence that civil commitment has "no discernible impact on the incidence of sex crimes"[18]—longtime critics of SVP laws such as Minnesota attorney Eric Janus, along with newer allies including the ACLU, have brought legal challenges to civil commitment and gotten positive rulings. In 2015, US District Judge Donovan W. Frank issued a scathing opinion in *Karsjens v. Piper*, declaring Minnesota's SVP law unconstitutional in practice: how could it claim to be therapeutic when in two decades not a single resident had been unconditionally released? "The overwhelming evidence at trial establishes that Minnesota's civil commitment scheme is a punitive system that segregates and indefinitely detains a class of potentially dangerous individuals without the safeguards of the criminal justice system," Frank wrote. In September 2016, citing similar evidence, a Missouri judge banned the lifetime detention of individuals who had served their sentences "no matter how heinous their past conduct."[19] The following year, a North Dakota court came to the same conclusion.[20]

But it was one step forward and two back. The Eighth Circuit Court of Appeals reversed Frank's ruling, and in 2018 the US Supreme Court denied a petition for review, leaving that opinion in place.[21] The federal district court in Missouri reversed its own ruling on the unconstitutionality of that state's law, citing the ultimate decision in *Karsjens*.[22] As this saga demonstrates, litigation that holds promise of progress for detainees in civil commitment may instead bring about the opposite; in this case, it became another brick in the wall of precedent against them.

Sex offender treatment has proven valuable for some participants. But whatever virtues any particular provider or program may possess, they are outweighed by the vices of the regime that oversees it. SOT perverts psychotherapy, a humane practice of self-exploration, into a compulsory, moralistic, and punitive exercise. Civil commitment does all that and more: it violates a slew of civil and human rights.

## Mental health without medicine: COSAs

To reject these punitive, medicalized models is not to suggest that people who have committed sexual harm be left to wander their neighborhoods without support from or accountability to others. In fact, one of the ironies of sex offender treatment is that while it supposedly aims to reeducate participants to relate differently to others, its terms and requirements, and the restrictions on registered citizens, foreclose almost all relationships, either casual or intimate: the offender must disclose his criminal status on the first date; he may not be in a room with children, including his family, even if his offense did not involve a child; he may not even chat with a teenager while waiting in line at the grocery store.

Happily, an increasing number of criminal legal systems around the country and the world offer nonmedical, community-based alternatives to SOT that have the potential to rebuild lives rather than destroy them with blame and shame. A circle of support and accountability, or COSA, is one such restorative practice. The circle consists of a person with convictions for what the state calls moderate to serious sex offenses (and other "violent crimes") who is recently released from prison, plus three or four community members, often including a paid coordinator. In weekly meetings and interim coffee, church, or basketball dates, the circle helps the "core member" with the basics of reentry, such as finding housing or applying for food stamps. By driving him to the supermarket or doing research online, they can ease the constraints of the registry (e.g., no driving, no Internet), reducing the odds he'll violate the terms of parole or probation.

The COSA assuages the isolation of people who are almost universally reviled. Starting with the nomenclature ("core member," not "perpetrator" or "offender"), participants model relationships of trust and mutual accountability informed by humanistic values; they treat the sex offender as a person worthy of affection, respect, and forgiveness. Equally important, they expect him to be accountable to them as a peer and an adult. According to sociologist Kathryn J. Fox, the COSA communicates to the former offender that he "shares the same moral space as ordinary citizens."[23]

The COSA is not just some flaky liberal experiment. It is a proven method of reducing harm. In Canada—where the program focuses on people who have been convicted of compulsive or violent sexual acts—COSAs have achieved a 70 percent reduction in recidivism.[24] In a study of 260 Vermont men released from prison, half with sex offenses, half without, those who had COSAs were convicted of new felonies at one-third the rate of a closely matched population who did not have COSAs.[25] Minnesota's COSAs lowered the "risk of rearrest for a new sex offense by 88 percent."[26]

Integrating COSAs into a criminal legal system allows them to be scaled up. But it also makes community members "employees" of the corrections department, which means they are expected to report the core member if they see him violating parole, say, by staying out after curfew or drinking a beer. For some potential participants, this is a deal-breaker—it is for us. In fact, it is contrary to the spirit of the COSA, which redefines accountability from "repaying your debt to society" by spending years inside a cage to showing up for other individuals and contributing to a community.

# 7

# "Real" Guilt and the Trouble with Innocence

When you talk about a person in prison or civil commitment, on parole or the registry, the first thing your interlocutor wants to know is what he was in for. When you tell them, the next question is "Did he do it?" In abolitionist and prisoners' rights circles, these questions are not relevant. There are numerous reasons: we do not want to classify people as the state does, with an identity marked by what might be the worst things they've done. We recognize that people's harmful actions happen in the context of violent systems and institutions, which have long been given a free pass. We know that innocent people, especially poor people of color, are falsely convicted in this system, which is stacked against them by economic inequality and racism. And we reject the dichotomy of perpetrator and victim. When rape or abuse is done, there is almost always enough trauma to go around, in the childhoods and adult lives of both harmed and harm-doer.

That said, we've met folks who have done terrible things: the man on the registry in Texas who sexually abused his stepdaughter for years beginning when she was four, even while she wept and begged him to stop; the serial rapist in civil commitment in California, one of whose victims testified that he told her she was no fun because she didn't scream and struggle; the New York State civil commitment resident who protested that he shouldn't be there because he was not a "sex offender." All he did was beat his ex-wife almost to death and slit her throat. Compared to these, many "sex offenders" look benign. Or innocent.

From these considerations we can tease out the arguments for and against harsh punishment, including the death penalty. On one side: some people are *really* guilty, the worst of the worst, and therefore deserve the worst we can give them. Against it: some people are innocent of the offense of which they were convicted, some because youth or intellectual or developmental disabilities rendered them unaware of their transgressions.

We reject both these arguments. Because if we are interested in securing something approaching justice—of an entirely different sort than what the criminal "justice" system delivers—a focus on statutory guilt or innocence leaves out too much of the story. Laws vary and change, reflecting, among many other things, the evanescent calculations and interests of policymakers and parties, political and religious constituencies, and corporate lobbies. And innocence and guilt are always unstable categories, tethered, as we've seen, to notions of race, class, gender, sexuality, ability, and maturity, which themselves change—and can be transformed—with politics, culture, and history.

## Child Saving

As an ensign in the battle against the punitive state, innocence is powerful. Beyond saving a person's life, advocates gain moral capital, and donor dollars, when they free a man who has been lingering on death row for thirty years after being railroaded by some corrupt sheriff. And beyond the man's individual persecution and exoneration, his face—the face of innocence—personifies the evils of a system and its credulous and ambitious prosecutors, "expert" witnesses, and judges, willing to destroy lives to advance careers or ideologies. Still, the concept of innocence itself must be unpacked and indicted for its role in obstructing justice and curtailing freedom.

The most compelling innocence claim, of course, is in the name of children—because the child is innocent by definition. In recent years, the notion of childhood innocence has cleansed even the Worst of the Worst Junior Division, "juvenile sex offenders." These reputedly incorrigible delinquents are being recast as promising, law-abiding heterosexual sons and fathers who made some youthful mistakes and deserve a second chance. For instance, a 2017 *New Yorker* article movingly profiled young people who ended up on the sex offender registry after being caught doing anything from playing doctor to sexually coercing another person.[1] And in 2015 the *New York Times* published a photograph of Zachary Anderson's parents on the front page, with a sympathetic story about their son, a white Indiana computer studies student who, at nineteen, had sex with a young woman who presented herself as seventeen but was really fourteen. He too faced sex offender registration.[2]

Several years after Human Rights Watch published *Raised on the Registry*, a 2013 report by lawyer and advocate Nicole Pittman that exposed the lifelong harms of the sex offender registration on youth, the national criminal legal reform advocacy organization Impact Justice established the Center on Youth Registration Reform (CYRR). The center's goal, according to its website, is "ending the abusive practice of placing children on registries." Earlier iterations of the tagline used the word "youth" instead of "children." That change plus the insertion of "abusive" amplify the message by evoking the innocence of childhood and the pain of child sexual abuse.

CYRR is one of a small number of organizations, including the Juvenile Law Center, and in some states the ACLU, that lobby and litigate to keep young people out of the clutches of the sex offense legal regime. They have a big job ahead of them. As of 2018, thirty-eight states included juveniles on sex offender registries;[3] as of 2015, fifteen posted their names and photos publicly.[4] Thirteen of the twenty states that confine people in civil commitment include detainees who committed their offenses as minors.[5] Thanks to these children's advocates, however, several states have ruled lifetime juvenile sex offender registration unconstitutional. The same arguments, reinforced by frequent reference to research showing that teenage brains aren't fully developed, have persuaded lawmakers and courts to eliminate the death penalty and reduce life without parole for those convicted as juveniles.

## Adult Abandonment

As a reform tactic, the appeal to innocence works. Yet it is also a dicey strategy, if the end goal is to dismantle the sex offense legal regime. For one thing, it was the (always racialized) notion of childhood innocence that sparked the sex panic to begin with. Consider the slogan *Believe the children*, which implied that children are too good to lie and encouraged credulity about the most outlandish fabricated claims of abuse by daycare workers. The child's presumed perfection exaggerates, by comparison, the wickedness of those who would sexually corrupt such a creature, and justifies the punishments meted out to them. In other words, the idea of innocence helped build the sex offense legal regime.

For another, replacing the term "juvenile offender" with "child" softens feelings about the young person, but it may also countenance the prosecution as an adult of any young person who is not perceived as childlike—more often the case if the child is not white. Campaigns that construct children as different from adults—more redeemable, more lovable—stir deserved sympathy for youth. Yet the public may just as easily be left feeling that adults who break the law are bad and deserve all they get. Similarly, a fixation on adult innocence is shadowed by unspoken indictments of the "truly guilty," preventing us from challenging a system that is equally unjust to them. Finally, political victories like the occasional exoneration of an innocent person or the achievement of a ban on registration of youth can fool us into thinking that the system is "broken," and merely needs a few fixes to work. In fact, the system *is* working. Its function is to police and punish. As activists, we must therefore choose: we can try to reform the system to do this job a little more fairly and a little less cruelly; or we can work to dismantle it.

Of course, children should be treated with care, both those who commit harm and those who experience it. The wrongfully convicted must be exonerated. Fortunately, the Innocence Project, a network of organizations that use DNA and other evidence to overturn such convictions, is doing just that. But we must build movements that do not collude with a system that deems only some people—due to age, race, sex, gender expression, sexuality, or criminal status—worthy of compassion, justice, and life. To dismantle the sex offense legal regime, moreover, we need to interrogate the meanings of sexual guilt in the United States and expose the sources of sex panic: attitudes toward children, sex, race, and Otherness.

# PART III

## Fractured Resistance

## *Racial or Gender or Class Justice?*

*[In the 1980s and '90s] political organizing strategies used by both anti-violence organizations and racial justice groups got co-opted by a "not-for-profit / social service" mentality that served as a distraction from the root causes of structural inequality and the violence that results from it. Groups organized to resist racialized oppression or class exploitation or gender violence or other monolithic formulations, treating them as separate issues. And they lost focus on how the state colludes to construct a hierarchy of oppression that cannot be agreed upon or changed.*

*On the ground today, it looks something like this. The anti-violence movement buys into the carceral state by advancing "anti-violence" campaigns that rely on arrest, prosecution, and punishment as ways to solve the problem of gender violence. The focus of the problem is individual incidents of abuse rather than public policies that result in state violence against women and queer communities, which are ignored by feminist groups who invest in or accept resources that are tied to the growing punishment industry. Those racial justice organizations that do resist state violence and the concomitant crises that result from mass incarceration see their work in masculinist terms. Some even point to anti-violence activism as one of the culprits in the mass incarceration of poor men of color. Many fail to understand that the criminal legal system is not only racist, it relies on heteropatriarchal assumptions that narrate a kind of social order that is based on domination.*

Beth E. Richie
abolitionist scholar
*Feminist Wire*, 2014[1]

In this passage from an essay called "How Anti-Violence Activism Taught Me to Become a Prison Abolitionist," Richie, a cofounder of INCITE!, elegantly describes one of the main reasons we wrote this book. Like her, we are distressed by the tendency of liberation struggles to splinter into narrowly focused enterprises that compete for grants and attention, undermining each other's efforts.

We know that not every conflict within or between movements is the product of political or personal shortsightedness. Some disputes stem from needs and interests that are at odds. Sometimes the distance between privilege and marginalization feels too great to bridge. Still, if we are to create the world we want, we need to struggle through these conflicts. That means examining the tensions and differentiating the ones that reflect fundamental differences in beliefs from those that merely indicate variations in strategies or tactics on the way to the same goal.

In Part III, we look at some of the movements that are addressing different aspects of the larger problem. We unpack persistent conflicts between them and identify points where alliances or coalitions might form. In so doing, we aim to find spaces where trust and relationships might grow, enabling individuals to work on the tougher stuff, and movements to build solidarity for the long haul.

# 8

# The "Registered Citizens'" Rights Movement

Over a decade ago, isolated and despised, a handful of people with convictions for sex offenses and their family members began to create small networks for mutual support and grassroots advocacy. Perhaps it is a sign of shame, perhaps simply of its diversity, but the members of these networks do not agree on what to call themselves. Sex offenders, SOs, registered citizens, persons with sex offense convictions—the list goes on. Lately, the term "registered citizens" is gaining traction. Still, the movement has no recognized name.

Yet fractious and fragile as it is, this collection of groups and networks has grown and matured, and attained the critical mass of a movement. We're calling it the registrants' rights movement, although it includes people in prison and civil commitment as well.

If any one person can be credited with launching this organizing, it is Paul Shannon, a longtime Boston peace and community activist, and—unlike many white, cisgender heterosexual men—a defender of demonized sexual minorities. In 1997, the kidnap and grisly murder of a white ten-year-old boy, Jeffrey Curley, by two men alleged to have ties to the North American Man/Boy Love Association (NAMBLA) sparked a witch hunt against "pedophiles" that threatened the entire Boston-area gay community and a call for a public sex offender registry in Massachusetts. Shannon circulated a petition opposing the registry on human and civil liberties grounds, collecting several hundred signatures from a wide variety of high-profile progressives. They did not prevail: the registry was instituted in 1999. Watching the panic grow and the laws worsen, in 2007 Shannon repurposed his petition into the essay "An Urgent Call to Support the Well-Being of Children and the Rights of Us All," which was published in *Counterpunch*.

Shannon's efforts galvanized the formation of Reform Sex Offender Laws (RSOL), which pulled together its first national conference in Boston that year. It later changed its name to National Association for Rational Sexual Offense Laws (NARSOL), to eliminate the use of the stigmatizing term "sex offender." NARSOL, according to Shannon, who is its chair, plays "a small but important part of the national debate" and provides a range of advocacy, legal activism, and member support. It organizes annual conferences and maintains an informative website; hosts call-ins and webinars on topics including legislation and legal cases, some of which it is involved in; and provides fellowship, including personal and inspirational testimony on its website and daylong, talk radio–like conference calls on Halloween and Christmas, when many registrants are alone.

At any given time, there are two or three dozen local groups alive, not all of them NARSOL affiliates. Their character and strategic emphases reflect their personnel and geography. Texas Voices for Reason and Justice, for instance, is steered by Mary Sue Molnar, whose background is in legislative politics makes her an effective lobbyist and whose patience and charisma help maintain an active board and keep members from despair. The executive director of California's Alliance for Constitutional Sex Offense Laws (ACSOL), Janice Bellucci, is a lawyer; accordingly, much of the group's activities center on litigation. When Bellucci sent notice of potential legal action against towns considering harsh residency restrictions, a number of the local governments deep-sixed the proposals rather than incur the costs of defending them. Illinois Voices For Reform has also built a strong platform for legislative work.

Early in the evolution of the movement, online hubs—CautionClick, Once Fallen, SOSEN (Sex Offender Solutions and Education Network)—popped up and were soon populated with news, forums, legal archives, and bibliographies. Any direct action they may have hoped to spark was limited, in part because so many people on the registry were forbidden to use the Internet. (This is changing. In 2017 in *Packingham v. North Carolina*, the

Supreme Court ruled that North Carolina's social media ban was a violation of registrants' free speech; state courts, including West Virginia's, have followed suit.)[1] A new entry on the scene, the Sex Offender Liberation Army (SOLA), appears to be one fed-up guy with a Twitter account.

Unfortunately, these groups' lobbying efforts sometimes scrape the sharp edges off the worst proposals, making them palatable enough to gain wider support among lawmakers—yet still bad for people with sex-related convictions. For example, California's ACSOL was a key actor in the 2017 amendment to the state's Sex Offender Registration Act that established three tiers of registrants based on the conviction and risk assessment, affecting the length and conditions of registration. At first glance this legislation looks like a win: it replaces a system that required, essentially, lifetime registration for the approximately 100,000 people on California's public registry. Yet the terms are still severe: ten years' registration for tier one, twenty for tier two, and lifetime registration for tier three. The legislation also placed everyone convicted of child pornography offenses on tier three and required a judge and the district attorney to authorize each removal from the registry. Most critically, the campaign left in place the assumptions underlying the registry, namely that some people *do* deserve to be on the list—just a smaller number, for less time.

As the most visible face of the movement, NARSOL is studiously moderate. It wants to "reform civil commitment processes"—not abolish civil commitment. It supports "removal of residency and proximity restrictions against registrants after their court-imposed sentence is satisfied"—but not complete repeal of restrictions that have no positive effect on public safety yet render thousands of registrants homeless. In fact, an activist in one local group told Judith that "everyone is against the registry and civil commitment," but making those positions public "would get us laughed off the map."

The registrants' movement has made impressive progress for a constituency living in near-constant fear of exposure, eviction, violence, and expulsion from jobs, community groups, and families. The movement has gotten a boost in the last few years, as a handful of other criminal justice and human rights activists, defense attorneys, academics, and civil libertarians has recognized the centrality of its issues and joined registered citizens in new activist and educational alliances such as the Sex Offender Policy Reform Initiative in Boston and the New York Sex Offense Working Group. The National Center for Reason and Justice (on whose board Judith serves) has long stood for the abolition of the sex offense legal regime.

The newly formed Legal Reform for People Intellectually and Developmentally Disabled has brought together scores of members nationally, mostly parents whose adult children have run afoul of sex offense laws, particularly those around child pornography. LRIDD's mission "is to ensure equal access to justice, [Americans with Disabilities Act] accommodations, and effective education and treatment for defendants with I/DD who are involved with the criminal justice system for sex-related offenses." As yet, the group has not drawn connections between its constituency's struggles and those of the millions of neurotypical individuals also ensnared by the regime.

## Challenging Civil Commitment

Of the whole sex offense legal regime, the civil commitment gulag may be the hardest to demolish. The courts continue to uphold the constitutionality of the sexually violent predator (SVP) laws, if not always their implementation. Because the institutions have been declared therapeutic and not criminal, patient privacy laws prevent journalists and activists from accessing information about who is inside. That allows authorities to keep circulating images of the "worst of the worst."

Nevertheless, challenges persist from outside the facilities' walls, as well as resistance from the residents within. Along with major cases such as 2015's *Karsjens v. Piper*, lawsuits flow from these institutions over constitutional violations and hellish conditions: guard brutality, solitary confinement, overcrowding, rotten food, negligent medical care, broken toilets, and on and on. Word of these lawsuits, some of which are brought by jailhouse lawyers, as well as political analysis, book reviews, and news from inside, is reported in the *Legal Pad*, an occasional newsletter produced by detainees of the Minnesota Sex Offender Program (MSOP) and distributed through the mail and by friends on the outside. The *Legal Pad*'s tone is by turns indignant and sardonic. For instance, a short item headlined "Two Recent Graduates" simply reproduces a portion of an official MSOP chart. The "graduation means" of two residents are listed as "complications from diabetes" and "unknown causes"—in other words, death.

### *Direct action*

In 2007 residents of Coalinga State Hospital in California went on strike to protest the conditions of their life imprisonment by refusing to participate in their sham "treatment." The protesters claimed to comprise three-quarters of the 600 men locked up there. A smaller contingent also went on hunger strike.

After eleven years of letters to the press, agency heads, and government officials, conference calls with legislative aides, and online posting of taped testimony of despondent residents raised no reaction, the people held at Coalinga took a different tactic: tax revolt. When the town of Coalinga put a sales tax increase to a local plebiscite, those incarcerated at the hospital saw an opportunity to trade their support for the tax for certain amenities, such as a van to the facility, which is far from town. The city officials ignored their entreaties, so the residents—who, unlike people in prison in most states, retain the right to vote—responded in kind. They built a vote-no campaign within the facility around the pennies the tax would add to the cost of a commissary hamburger, and defeated the tax by a few dozen votes. Not by coincidence, town officials subsequently claimed there was a pornography "epidemic" at the facility and locked it down, confiscating electronic devices and shredding residents' legal and medical records. ACSOL Executive Director Bellucci sued to get the residents' belongings back, but it was too late: most had already been destroyed.

At this writing, a Coalinga resident is running for city council as a write-in. The mayor and council chair have arbitrarily declared his candidacy illegitimate.

### *Reformists and radicals*

Outside the gates, friends and families of people in civil commitment have assumed roles that range from protesters to lobbyists to citizen participants in the governance of the facilities. For instance, since about 2013, Kansas's SPTP Friends and Families—which advocates for people held in the state's Sexual Predator Treatment Program (SPTP)—has built alliances with psychologists and disability rights advocates, particularly the local chapter of the National Alliance on Mental Illness. The chapter's then-director, Rick Cagan, was appalled that Kansas was pouring 60 percent of its shrinking mental health budget into the SPTP; by 2017 total costs were approaching $300 million. "At the outset it may have some public purpose in terms of public safety, but from all of our analysis it is not a program that has any integrity," Cagan said. "There's a front door but no back door to the institution."

One of the leaders of Friends and Families also coordinates a national civil commitment network, including residents, which meets in a monthly conference call under the aegis of the prisoners' rights organization Citizens United for Rehabilitation of Errants (CURE). But Friends and Families has not moved to shutter the SPTP facility. Instead, it submitted a long position paper to the legislature asking for "fixes to deficiencies" in the program, such as regularized and legible treatment levels, better staffing, and more visiting days, and has worked with state agencies to implement them. For now, at least, it appears that the organization has chosen to oil the parts, not smash the machine.

Probably the only mental health patients' rights group with an uncompromising stance toward civil commitment is Mental Health America, a mainstream advocacy organization founded in 1909. Its position is straightforward: "Sexual predator laws should be repealed." Until that happens, MHA demands that the state be "even more vigilant" and "provide heightened procedural protections for sex offender commitments."[2]

These activists are negotiating the tension between reform and radical action—between petitions for increased staffing and hunger strikes fundamentally challenging the institution of civil commitment. This tension burst through the phone lines during one of the CURE-facilitated monthly civil commitment conference calls. Listening as resident representatives reported, one by one, the same conditions they'd reported the month before and the month before that, one woman—the mother of a young man with a mentally disability who is locked up in Illinois—could no longer contain her exasperation. "I thought we were going to shut these fucking things down," she shouted, "not just talk about how bad they are!"

Like other movements of the families of incarcerated people, the one advocating for the inmates of civil commitment improves the lives of folks on the inside by agitating for better food, medical care, and the like. But such activities as pressuring governments for more rational protocols in treatment plans that defy reason and demanding a say in devising procedures in oppressive SVP programs can cross the line from constructive criticism to collaboration. We agree with the woman on the conference call. The correct goal is to shut the fucking things down.

## Conflicts

### *"Sex offender" movements versus racial justice activists: Mutual erasure*

"The whitest group of criminal justice reformers? The people working to challenge the registry and support sex offenders," Tammy Bond told Erica, over pancakes in a Chicago diner. Bond is a registrant and an organizer with Illinois Voices for Reform, a statewide network founded in 2010 whose mission is "the elimination of sexual abuse and the preservation of civil rights for all individuals through the use of effective legislation based on empirical research."

While Bond is typical in her experience as a person convicted of a sex offense—she struggles to find housing and employment and is often shunned once someone learns of her offense—she is atypical in other critical ways. As an African American woman, she navigates the registrants' rights movement with what W. E. B. Du Bois, in *The Souls of Black Folk*, called a "double consciousness"—or a triple one.

In the restaurant, Bond's voice drops as she says the words "sex offenders," eyes sliding to the next table, where small children throng around the adults. She recounts a recent meeting on SO issues where she and an elected official with a strong history of criminal justice reform work were two of the only Black people in a room full of white faces. That meeting was not unique. Virtually the entire leadership and membership of the registrants' movement are white. At the same time, the organizers and rank and file of movements against the prison industrial complex are largely of color.

Why is the registrants' rights movement so white? In part it's because the organizers' social networks are almost exclusively white, with a concentration in Southern white evangelical churches. But that observation begs the question. Perhaps a better explanation is that people with convictions for sex offenses often do not see themselves as criminals—they are more likely to insist they are innocent of their charges or were convicted of acts that should not be illegal, such as consensual sex with a teenager.

In individual cases, these claims may be true. But it is a time-honored political move to represent oneself as unstained by criminality; indeed, Latinx groups during the 2004 mobilizations to legalize undocumented migrants used the slogan *Yo no soy criminal*. It is also a racialized one. "Criminality" is naturalized, one of the rationales, for instance, of eugenics. Distancing from the symbolic markers of criminality is also a move away from Blackness. Where sex offenses are concerned, *white boys will be boys. But Black boys will be criminals.*

To identify as a part of the movement against mass incarceration would also be to embrace what has become one of its core analyses: Michelle Alexander's *New Jim Crow*, which posits mass incarceration as the most recent chapter—following chattel slavery,

Reconstruction, lynching, Jim Crow, and legalized segregation—in an uninterrupted, deliberate suppression of the freedom, rights, and economic well-being of Black people. For white registrants, to join forces with the anti-prison movement would mean assuming a kind of kinship with Black folk, and acknowledging that in spite of the depredations they suffer as "predators," they still enjoy what Du Bois called "the public and psychological wage" of whiteness.[3]

There are, however, exceptions to this stark racial division. Texas Voices for Reason and Justice, for instance, identifies itself with the broader prison reform movement, as "a statewide, nonprofit, volunteer organization devoted to promoting a more balanced, effective, and rational criminal justice system." Through it, wives and mothers (and a few fathers) of people convicted of sexual offenses regularly attend the Texas Inmate Families Association, an organization whose membership is racially diverse. In Missouri, Women Against Registry (WAR) put in at least one appearance at a Black Lives Matter march. And the community of registrants around Boston's Sex Offender Policy Reform Initiative has about an equal number of white men and men of color.

Illinois Voices for Reform's website is unique in foregrounding structural inequalities in the criminal legal system. Its home page notes that while "1 in 227 men in Illinois is labeled a 'sex offender,' the rate is about 1 in 100 for African-American men," and that "reciprocal connections between [sex offender] registration and poverty, racism, and disability have been unexplored, and the impact of social exclusion unaddressed. Current laws tend to stigmatize and debilitate families, and make it difficult for service providers to address re-entry, unemployment, homelessness, mental health treatment and other collateral consequences."

The wider criminal justice reform movement has not exactly welcomed sex offenders either. Bond recalls a national convention for formerly incarcerated people whose attendees were almost all Black. In dozens of sessions involving hundreds of attendees, no one publicly identified as a sex offender and no SO issues were raised. Bond approached the convener, a Black formerly incarcerated man, and introduced herself as someone with a conviction for a sex offense. Why was no one talking about that? she asked. His response: *We never thought about it.*

Nearly 900,000 people on public registries in the United States, and he never thought about it? He was probably telling the truth. For him, those people are invisible.

Revulsion against "child molesters" and "predators" cannot be discounted as a factor in this effacement. Incarcerated people and their advocates already have to contend with the stereotypes of ruthless gangsters and murderers; who needs another monster on the roster? At the same time, the anti-carceral movement rejects identifying people by the criminal labels the state affixes; a person who has been convicted of homicide is not viewed as part of a category called "murderers." Finally, just as the registrants' movement fails to acknowledge the historic white supremacy of which the criminal legal system is part, for mobilizations against mass incarceration that place their struggle within a New Jim Crow framework, the perceived whiteness of the sexual "predator" does not fit.

## *Criminal legal reform versus "sex offender" rights: Florida Amendment 4*

"Everyone deserves a second chance. *Everybody*," said the narrator, who sounds like a boomer-generation African American man, in a video promoting the Second Chances Campaign of the Florida Rights Restoration Coalition (FRRC). "Floridians from all walks of life believe in forgiveness, redemption, restoration and, ultimately, second chances," read the Second Chances website. The four-year, $16 million campaign was pressing for the Voting Rights Restoration Amendment—Amendment 4 of the state constitution—automatically restoring voting rights to people with felony convictions. Historically, Florida had disenfranchised ex-felons for life. They could get their rights back, but only through a clemency board, which rarely awarded approvals. The state's 1.6 million disenfranchised felons—a quarter of the nation's 6 million—represented one in ten voting-age Floridians, but one in five potential voters who are Black.

More than three-quarters of a million Floridians signed the petition to get the amendment on the ballot. Endorsers ranged from Bernie Sanders to John Legend, Vietnam vets to Tampa Bay rabbis, the *Miami Herald* to the *Harvard Law Review*. On Election Day 2018, 60 percent of voters approved the amendment.

But Amendment 4 does not give *everybody* a second chance. "No person convicted of murder or a felony sex offense shall be qualified to vote until restoration of civil rights," it reads.[4] The ACLU, which drafted it, ran focus groups to see what would fly, and learned that Floridians were not sanguine about allowing "predators" back into the precincts of citizenship. At a meeting of the Florida Action Committee, the state's registrants' rights organization, FRRC Executive Director Desmond Meade reportedly explained: "Nobody likes child molesters." In media interviews Meade reassured audiences that the worst criminals would be hard pressed ever to cast a ballot in Florida.

The campaign for Amendment 4 illuminates the choices criminal justice activists face when they opt for partial reform over thoroughgoing change. It illustrates as well the challenges those decisions pose to organizers for the rights of people convicted of sex offenses.

To get bills through recalcitrant legislatures, criminal legal system reformers grab at the most convenient—and proven effective—bargaining chip: sex offenders. That's what sponsors of the bipartisan First Step federal criminal justice reform bill did in 2018. The national Uniform Law Commission excluded sex offenders while negotiating for consensus on its 2010 model Uniform Collateral Consequences of Conviction Act. The UCCCA requires a state to apprise criminal defendants pre-plea of the hundreds of restrictions a felony conviction imposes on an ex-offender and provides an avenue to getting those limits lifted. People with sex convictions face the most severe collateral consequences of exposure on the public registry, including murder.

Civil libertarians have been known to equivocate on the rights of people with sex-related convictions. In 1990, when the Washington State Legislature was conducting hearings on the Community Protection Act—the mother of civil commitment and community notification—the state's ACLU declined to testify, concluding that "it would be counterproductive, with emotions running so high," according to the *Los Angeles Times*.[5] In 2018, when Secretary of Education Betsy DeVos amended Title IX campus sexual assault regulations to safeguard some due process rights of the accused, the ACLU abandoned its mission to defend the Fifth Amendment and announced that DeVos's new rule "inappropriately tips the scales in favor of the accused."[6]

When criminal justice reform bills are being debated and promoted, people convicted of sex offenses are faced with either defending themselves and endangering the chances of reform, or going along with the reform at their own expense. Aside from Florida's SO rights group, only one progressive organization opposed Amendment 4: the Human Rights Defense Center, a venerable advocate for people locked up in every kind of penal institution in the United States, from juvenile detention to military brigs. A longtime opponent of the private prison industry, HRDC is also the publisher of *Prison Legal News*.

HRDC acknowledged Amendment 4 as a positive development for some oppressed people. Yet, in a public statement, it condemned the harm obscured by the campaign's propaganda. "All the talk of Amendment 4 supporters about second chances, redemption, reintegration into the community, etc. rings hollow and opportunistic when they made the decision to exclude murderers and sex offenders from the franchise," said the statement. It warned that by depriving two specific categories of persons of a voice in electoral politics, Amendment 4 would "enshrine bigotry and discrimination" in the state constitution and "enable even greater discrimination against [those people] in areas such as housing, education, [and] government benefits." HRDC noted that it was unlikely that a multimillion-dollar campaign would arise to restore the excluded groups' voting rights anytime soon. The statement continued:

> For twenty-eight years, HRDC has advocated on behalf of all people negatively impacted by the criminal justice system,

> including sex offenders and murderers. We have never pitted one impoverished, oppressed and vulnerable population against another and, more importantly, we have never advocated for nor sought to advance the rights of any person or constituency to the detriment or loss of rights of any other person or constituency.

In declining to join the coalition for Amendment 4, HRDC invoked the rallying cry *All of us or none*—which is also the name of a grassroots organization made up of currently and formerly incarcerated people. As HRDC Executive Director Paul Wright put it in an op-ed in the *Florida Times-Union*, "You can't fight discrimination and bigotry by perpetuating it."[7]

The passage of Amendment 4 with a large majority was met with joy by many who see it as a victory in the struggle to challenge racism and rebuild electoral democracy, at a time of aggressive voter suppression of people of color and the poor. But those of us who have also struggled against the sex offense legal regime recognize this campaign's political expediency—or cynicism—as depressing old news. Once again, the rights of some have been given away for a "greater good."

The same happened in the nineteenth century when conflict arose between white women suffragists and abolitionists fighting for the right of African American men to vote. Accepting that the two groups could not simultaneously win their rights, their leaders split, denouncing one another. The Fifteenth Amendment, granting Black men the vote, was ratified in 1869. (It was soon supplanted in the South by Jim Crow laws that revoked those rights, in part by rampant false criminal convictions of Black men, whose franchise could then be denied based on criminal status.) It took fifty years for white women to get the vote, and almost a hundred for the passage of the federal Civil Rights and Voting Rights Acts in 1964 and 1965. And Black people still face voter suppression. Solidarity failed, and racism and sexism won.

### *Mainstream LGBTQ advocates versus "sex offenders": "Too controversial"*

It's something of an irony that the Los Angeles–based LGBTQ film festival Outfest awarded its Documentary Grand Jury Prize to *Southwest of Salem: The Story of the San Antonio Four*, an affecting film by Deborah Esquenazi about the struggle to prove the innocence of four Chicana lesbians—dubbed the San Antonio Four—wrongly convicted in 1995 of the sexual assault of two girls.

The state and the press deployed the defendants' Otherness—queerness, brownness, poverty—to convict them. In court the prosecutor mentioned their lesbianism dozens of times. The alleged abuse, a local investigative journalist says in the film, sounded "like a porn movie—a man's version of what women do in their spare time."[8] Yet the people who could, and should, have come to the women's aid during their fifteen-year ordeal ran the other way—including LGBTQ organizations.

It wasn't the first time. LGBTQ advocates were nowhere to be found in 1984, when Bernard Baran, a young, white, working-class gay Massachusetts daycare worker, was arrested on false child abuse charges stemming unambiguously from a parent's homophobia.[9] They were AWOL a few years later, when Margaret Kelly Michaels, another teacher, was indicted on 115 of 163 counts of abuse that included putting knives and forks in toddlers' vaginas and forcing them to eat cake made of feces. Her lesbian relationship figured prominently in her prosecution, too.[10]

The distance between the queer advocate and the sex offender was painfully evident in 2014 when Laverne Cox, Black feminist star of the Netflix series *Orange Is the New Black* and longtime advocate for transgender folks in prison, backed away from the End Solitary campaign. That project was instigated by a New York–based anti-poverty and transgender legal advocacy organization, the Sylvia Rivera Law Project (SLRP), which works to expose the treatment of trans people in prison. The reason for Cox's change of heart: news sources revealed that one person the campaign sought to support, Synthia China Blast, was in prison for convictions including child sexual abuse and was therefore marked, according to *The Advocate*, as "too controversial." SLRP was not deterred by Cox's public withdrawal from the campaign. "Supporting any individual person is not about pardoning their crime, but about protecting the rights of all incarcerated people and ending the use of systematic torture as 'punishment,' " the group wrote in a 2014 statement about this incident.[11] Unfortunately, SLRP is an outlier in their consistent support for trans and queer people who are criminalized, regardless of the conviction.

Though not excusable, mainstream LGBTQ advocates' reluctance to go near any "sex offender" is understandable. Queers have long been charged with sexually preying on children. Best not to draw attention to anyone who might seem to confirm that myth—especially now, as LGBTQ respectability politics grows increasingly preoccupied with marriage, military service, and mommying and daddying. Or so the thinking goes. This mainstream has remained largely unmoved even by the most egregious examples of state violence against the most vulnerable of the LGBTQ community, such as police brutality visited on people committing the crime of "walking—or driving, dining, shopping standing—while trans." It is notable that the San Antonio Four, convicted of sexually harming children, were not embraced until their innocence was secure and widely known.

Still, keeping "sex offenders" at arm's length has a cost to every LGBTQ person—most of all, ironically, to those who long to move to the suburbs and join the PTA. In 2009, Erica noted that no mainstream LGBTQ organization had "initiated any public campaigns or research about how [sex offender registries] could potentially augment 'fear of the queer' by recirculating public discourses on 'sex offenders.' " In fact, by refusing to defend—and actively ostracizing—the queerest among them, she said, mainstream lesbian and gay organizations perpetuate their own "fear of the queer."[12]

## Potential Alliances: "All of Us or None"

These disparate movements—registrants' rights, prison abolitionism, and LGBTQ—can educate and support each other, fortifying their separate efforts while building toward more holistic, radical, far-reaching transformations.

The registered citizens' movement can learn a lot from policing and prison abolitionists, who are, as a group, more experienced organizers with developed political analyses. Registrants might be emboldened to move beyond a reformist agenda and call for abolition of the sex offender registry and civil commitment. Meanwhile, opponents of the carceral state hearing from people under the control of the sex offense legal regime might better anticipate some of the system's next moves and their effects, such as the broadening use of risk assessment and electronic surveillance technologies, or the putatively therapeutic civil commitment of "sexually violent predators" as a precursor of the repackaging of jails and prisons as "mental health care" facilities—what African studies researcher and organizer James Kilgore calls "carceral humanism."[13] As for LGBTQ people and those statutorily designated as criminal deviants, the system and the mainstream public persist in lumping them together, so they might as well work together against their common oppressors. And all these groups can offer each other close-up insights into the oppressions that undergird the carceral edifice—whether those of race, sex, gender, citizenship, occupation, or criminal status. With this experience and mutual understanding, organizers can muster the political will and power to withstand pressure to trade away the rights of the most despized.

Seen this way, the Human Rights Defense Center, in distancing itself from Amendment 4, was not a political spoiler in a righteous campaign or an intransigent holdout for some unattainable political purity. Rather, HRDC was demonstrating its commitment to building movements that do not turn on the disposability of the marginalized. The organization is not alone. JustLeadershipUSA, founded in 2014 with the goal of halving the number of people in prison by 2030, explicitly included people with a diverse range of convictions, sex offenses among them, in its signature initiative: a leadership program for formerly incarcerated people called Leading with Conviction. "We are not going to solve the problems of mass incarceration by focusing on nonviolent, non-felony, non-sex crimes or by paying too much attention to laws that only support first-time offenders," said its policy and campaigns director.[14]

Black and Pink, founded in 2004, is the world's largest organization for incarcerated people who identify as LGBTQ. It has over 10,000 participants both inside and outside prison. In 2016, when a letter-writer to its newsletter balked at the organization's support for people with sex offenses, founder Jason Lydon responded in his column:

> As a reminder, Black and Pink is open to working with all LGBTQ prisoners, regardless of what they are convicted of. We are not here, as a family, to cast anyone out because of their actions. We are not defining any person as only one action. All of us are more than the worst thing we have ever done. We also recognize that not everyone did the things they were convicted of. We also know that what people are convicted of is not always the worst thing they have done. We honor all of these things to be true. This does not mean, though, that we ignore the harm each other have caused.[15]

A daylong LGBTQ-focused convening in December 2018 offered a glimpse of the promise of usually unconnected (or even antagonistic) players coming together. A cluster of organizations that make up the National LGBT/HIV Criminal Justice Policy Working Group gathered in Washington, DC. In the room were lawyers from leading LGBTQ legal rights organizations such as Lambda Legal; policy directors from national organizations like Queeri, which advocates for queer people of color; and some queer and criminal justice scholars (Erica included). A key feminist anti-violence organizer Skyped in.

Such a meeting might have been unexceptional, but for two things: the topic of the day—sex offense policy, and how and why LGBTQ folks might be overrepresented in this criminal category;

and the other attendees—people on the registry and their allies, including Women Against Registry (WAR), which has declared feminists the enemy.

Also symbolic of the meeting's potential was that it took place at the national office of the Human Rights Campaign, the largest and best-funded mainstream LGBTQ organization in the United States. HRC has no history of pushing back against policing or prisons, or of joining efforts to raise the visibility of queer folk entangled in the system. For a decade the organization trained its sights on one goal—marriage equality—getting in bed with anyone who'd endorse legalizing same-sex unions, including anti-choice and pro-punishment electoral candidates. Not to assign too much meaning to the use of a conference room, but the welcome of this nascent radical alliance by this assiduously middle-of-the-road organization sparked a question: might the mainstream and the margins come together on an issue that has frightened organizers across the political spectrum? HRC even paid for lunch.

*All of us or none* is not only a moral statement; it is a strategic guideline. In fact, the necessity of forfeiting some people's rights to attain others' may be more perceived than real. Californians who sued in 2016 for the voting rights of people in jail, serving time for misdemeanors, or under community supervision did not peel off any criminal population from their demands. They won judicial approval, popular support, and the legislation they sought.[16]

To create a much-needed alliance to defeat the prison industrial complex and dismantle its egregious sex offense legal regime, movements need an intersectional analysis and a willingness to undertake the hard work of building solidarity across difference. SO rights advocates must cease clinging to whiteness. Anti-prison organizers must resist the pull of sexual moralism and the push of sexual repugnance. And queers must not succumb to sexual McCarthyism, seeking safety and respectability by renouncing others more "despicable" than themselves.

# 9

# Religious Movements: Redemption, with Conditions

New Name Ministries is a residence in the Dallas–Fort Worth area for sex offenders released from prison. Its director, Jon Cordiero, former president of NARSOL and also a board member of Texas Voices for Reason and Justice, is a fundamentalist pastor, and the residence is explicitly Christian. New Name's first "statement of faith" is: "The Bible is without mistakes as originally given, and God inspired the words." Among the criteria for admission that applicants are asked to affirm is "I have committed my whole life to Jesus Christ."

If you are coming out of prison with a sex offense, in much of the country the only folks you can turn to are Christian evangelicals. The same is true inside US prisons. As secular rehabilitative and educational programs have lost political support, unpaid "faith-based" groups have moved in to take their place, offering everything from AA to GEDs. "In many states, nondenominational Protestant Christians make up more than 85 percent of the volunteers who enter the prison," allowing "massive numbers of Christians to enter and proselytize to those desperate for a lifeline," writes religion and gender studies scholar Tanya Erzen in *God in Captivity: The Rise of Faith-Based Prison Ministries in the Age of Mass Incarceration*.[1]

That lifeline can be literal. At Hutchins State Jail in Fort Worth, the only air-conditioned space aside from the lobby and the offices is the chapel. So it is no wonder that on the August evening Judith visited with Restoration Outreach of Dallas (ROD) Ministries' Reverend Jeffrey Parker and his deacons, at least one hundred men filed in. Every summer across the South, prison inmates become ill or die from the heat.[2]

What born-again Christians believe in most fervently is

redemption: every person has God, or good, within; no one is identical to their wrongdoings; and everyone can be washed clean of sin and restored to righteousness. The ministries that embrace SOs eschew the state's language of irreparability. Cordiero, for one, refuses to use the term "sex offender." In a system that locks people up or puts them on registries for life, and a culture in which many consider a sex-related offense unforgiveable, faith in redemption is a rarity—and precious.

Yet the relationship between these churches and sexual harm is vexed. They call out to men who have sinned to come, repent, and be reborn. They proselytize that to walk with God is to walk away from crime. But, in fact, adherence to orthodox religion is correlated with sexual offending, and not just among clergy. A study of freshmen at a Southern US university found that "those who had been sexually abused by a relative were much more likely to be affiliated with fundamental[ist] Protestant religions."[3] And a 2006 study of religiosity among Australian men incarcerated for serious sex offenses found that those who maintained religious involvement from childhood to adulthood had more sexual offense convictions, more victims, and younger victims than other groups, including atheists.[4] Among Jewish men in an Israeli prison, "religious Jews . . . were more likely to be in for sex crimes," according to other research.[5] And of course the evidence of decades, maybe centuries, of sexual abuse of children and women by "celibate" Catholic priests reveals the dangers inherent in authoritarian patriarchal institutions whose clergy are believed to have exclusive access to God, and which administer their worldly business in secret with little public accountability.

There is no major institutional religion that is not patriarchal, and too many religious institutions and individual churches, synagogues, mosques, or ashrams tacitly condone violence against children and women, including corporal punishment and marital rape, as well as cruelty toward LGBTQ people. Readings of religious law by ultraorthodox Jewish sects, for instance, cast women's bodies—even their voices—as temptations to men to sin. And "as it is the men who both write, read, and interpret the rules of Judaism, Orthodox women are subject to their husband's or father's chosen interpretation, which could be to their benefit or to their peril," wrote social service administration professor Meredith Blackman in *Advocates Forum* in 2010.[6] That peril may find the form of domestic violence or sexual abuse.

While sanctioning male heterosexual aggression, the same doctrines also censure a wide range of nonviolent, consensual acts and identities, including child sex play, nonmarital sex, pornography, prostitution, and—most virulently—homosexuality. "We believe the Bible is pretty clear on homosexuality," New Name Ministry's administrative director told Judith. "Sin is not that fun, naughty thing. It's destructive, a deviation from God's design."

In *God in Captivity*, Erzen tells the poignant story of Chandra, imprisoned at the Louisiana Correctional Institution for Women, where a Baptist theology degree is the only opportunity for higher education. To enter the program, Chandra had to renounce her lesbianism. Once admitted, she was schooled to see her sexuality as the cause of her crimes, which included the murder of her lover. Chandra grew disgusted with her butch appearance and worked to alter it. Unable to change her sexuality, she became celibate and started an ex-gay ministry in the prison. "I want the ladies to become not just heterosexual but to become holy," she told Erzen.[7] Under fundamentalist Baptism, if you're queer, the choice is clear: your desire or your salvation.

In the course of our advocacy and research, we have become close to some ultraconservative Christians in the registrants' rights movement. We know them to be deeply ethical people, trying to live in the image of Jesus. But as activists, they negotiate a thicket of contradictions. They oppose the registry yet embrace the sexual values that inform the laws that put people on it. We often meet men who feel they deserve punishment, if not perdition, for dubiously harmful acts, such as talking online to an agent posing as a middle-school girl. Theirs is a social justice movement that asks for acceptance of people who have transgressed society's rules. Yet many of its evangelical members subscribe to radical intolerance in both private and public life.[8]

The sex offense legal regime is a reflection of a vengeful, sexist, and homophobic culture. A movement to abolish those policies cannot do so when its members are implicated in perpetuating that culture, even in the name of love and redemption.

## Potential Alliances: Sacred and Secular, Conservative and Progressive

Religion is interpretation. Millions of the faithful interpret the scripture and doctrine of their religions as commanding them to work for social justice. *Tikkun olam* (Heal the world) is a Jewish dictum. Religious women from Fannie Lou Hamer to Linda Sarsour have figured their faith as central to liberation movements. The African American Orthodox Jew Yavilah McCoy is a trusted leader in forging intersectional partnerships. And one of our most radical comrades, Black and Pink founder Jason Lydon, is a queer Unitarian minister. A lineage of organizers and activists for prison and death penalty abolition, immigrants' rights, peace, economic and racial justice, and reproductive justice and feminism hear the call to struggle for freedom—leaving no one behind—in the words of liturgy.

For those of us committed to restorative and transformative justice, as for many religious folks, the concepts of accountability and redemption shape our worldview and our daily practice. Through these practices we are creating new secular languages of error and rebirth, new stories in which the redeemer is not a messiah or a saint, but ourselves and our communities. At the same time, in challenging sexual violence and the ideologies that support it, we cannot ignore the principle meaning-maker for millions of people: almost eight in ten Americans say that religion is very or somewhat important in their daily lives.[9] In fact, in many communities, religious congregations present a great opportunity for organizing, because that's where the people are.

But while the devout have long worked in secular movements for social justice, few progressive secular organizations venture into more conservative religious communities—or are trusted by those communities—especially with the mission of addressing sexual violence. The Harlem-based anti-violence organization

CONNECT is one of these few. Through its Faith Circle and its work within individual congregations, it partners with both clergy and laity to address and prevent interpersonal violence within and around the church. Along the way, CONNECT provides entryways for parishioners—often women who have experienced or witnessed sexual violence—to look at the patriarchal beliefs that undergird gender violence, including those in their own churches.

"You have to tenderly go in and work on a very consistent basis," says CONNECT codirector and ordained minister Sally MacNichol. "What were their own experiences? What do they see in the church? What do these scriptures sound like, vis-à-vis someone who is being abused or is abusing?" And, she asks them to consider, is it possible to change their churches, and if so, how? When change is not forthcoming, some parishioners feel compelled to leave the church. But they do not want to leave a faith they love. CONNECT helps them create spaces between: "side ministries" that support victims of interpersonal violence within a context of worship.

"There's always been a lot of animosity between feminism and faith," MacNichol says. "The more patriarchal the situation, the more violence there's going to be." But over months and years, religious people committed to understanding sex and gender violence "start to see things in a different way. It's inevitable."

# 10

# Men Face Masculinity

"You can't talk about violence without talking about manhood, and you can't talk about manhood without talking about violence," Jackson Katz told *Bitch* magazine.[1] Katz is one of the best-known American men to work with other men to challenge masculine violence.

It may seem an obvious statement. And in the past couple of decades, more and more men have developed organizations and programs to encourage and train other men and boys to be better men. Men are talking about manhood and violence. But what are they saying? That makes all the difference.

## Anti-violence and Anti-feminist

On one end of the spectrum are right-wing religious groups like the forty-year-old evangelical missionary Christian Men's Network, whose Global Fatherhood Initiative travels the world teaching men "to be servant-leaders to their families, churches, and culture, and challenges men to keep their word, become responsible fathers, faithful husbands, and men of character—Christlike men." CMN unashamedly trumpets its white supremacy and cultural imperialism. For instance, its website boasts, "Uganda: Alex engaged the men of a backward, immoral, polygamist nation, the epicenter of the AIDS epidemic, and taught them sexual morality and marital fidelity."

Programs like CMN—along with the evangelical Christian Promise Keepers and Muslim minister Louis Farrakhan's Million Man March—preach that God gave men a special duty to protect and guide women and children, which also means enforcing the rule of (patriarchal) law in the family, the community, and house of worship. For these men, there's nothing wrong with male supremacy, except that men aren't upholding it vigorously enough: a Promise Keepers' T-shirt reads "Man Up!" To their exhortations to machismo, these anti-violence preachers add one caveat: Rule, but rule with respect. CONNECT's Sally MacNichol paraphrases: "Be a benevolent dictator."

We are skeptical of a plan to end child sexual abuse by installing a strong father in every home. After all, it is male family and household members who commit most abuse of children and women.

## A Kinder, Gentler Masculinity

### *Dancing with patriarchs*

It can be tough to challenge male violence within patriarchy without denouncing patriarchal institutions or subcultures. Danny Salim directs the anti-violence program at the Arab-American Family Support Center in New York City, which contracts with the city to provide counseling for families affected by domestic violence. He defines relationships as either healthy, unhealthy, or abusive. A healthy relationship is one of "mutual trust and respect, with equal power." In an unhealthy one, the partners make each other miserable, but equally. And in an abusive relationship, "one person has all the power and the other has no power"; the powerful partner controls the other, emotionally, physically, or financially.

"What about the family structure where the man heads the household, earns and controls the money, and makes all the decisions for the women and children?" Judith asked Salim.

"You're describing the patriarchal family," he replied.

"That sounds like what you call an abusive relationship. Is there such a thing as a healthy patriarchal relationship?" And is such a relationship a product of a patriarchal system or cultural?

Salim answered: "We see [masculine hyper-control] as a misunderstanding, a misconception of one's role in one's culture—by the individual," he said. "We wouldn't blame it on the whole community, because each person is unique." Are patriarchal roles therefore okay, but just misunderstood and misused? Is culture so weak that individuals can opt in or out as they please? Perhaps Salim's job as a counselor and mediator precludes taking a stance on the family structures of many of his clients. But that seems to trap him between cultural critique and cultural sensitivity, between the political and what may be an overly tolerant interpretation of the personal.

Similarly, there's a limit to how far you can go in anti-violence work without rejecting the principal institutions of masculine domination. In reaction to spates of accusations from enlisted women of sexual assault and harassment perpetrated by their male peers and officers, the US military has engaged trainers, including Katz, to conduct gender violence prevention and bystander intervention.[2] Like the prevention of child abuse through the promotion of authoritarian fatherhood, anti-violence training with men whose job is to kill people—the epitome of toxic masculinity—is an oxymoron. These military projects also carry a strong whiff of Othering: soldiers should be respectful of "our" women, and even refrain from raping "enemy" women and girls, but it's okay to kill their fathers, brothers, or husbands and, if necessary, to blow up their homes and cities.

These efforts are not working. Biannual Pentagon surveys show a steady increase in sexual assaults and harassment at military academies. "This isn't a blip, a #MeToo bump, or some accident," averred California Democrat Jackie Speier at a February 2019 House subcommittee hearing. "It's a clear illustration of a destructive trend and systemic problem."[3]

## *Brothers and sisters*

Unions have done some interesting work around sexual harassment that invites men to see women as humans like themselves, albeit without rocking the ship of gender. After conducting a survey of 487 female hotel and casino workers on their experiences of sexual harassment, the Hands Off Pants On campaign of Chicago's Unite Here Local 1 produced a video aimed at potential male harassers. In the video, a half dozen union men read the women's testimony. "I do not feel safe because of the things I have encountered. One guest was masturbating," reads a mail carrier, pausing at the word before going on. A metal worker reads: "I was seven months pregnant. I felt so disgusted and embarrassed." He adds his own commentary: "Pigs."

The men look into the camera in disbelief, disgust, or shame. Then they connect the women's experiences to their own family loyalties. "I have four daughters. I have sisters. I have nieces." "If my sister or my daughter were subjected to this, there would be some violent action taken." The comments are paternalistic, macho—attitudes in the same range of the male privilege that produces sexual abuse. But uttering the women's words awakens empathy as fellow humans, and, as union brothers, solidarity with their union sisters.

## Deconstructing Gender—to a Point

The anti-violence educator Keith Edwards, who is white, and Call to Men, the organization led by Tony Porter and Ted Bunch, both African American, use the metaphor of the "man in a box" to illustrate how masculinity is confining and suffocating, both to men and to women. "In the man box," says Call to Men, "women are objects, the property of men, and of less value than men. The teachings of the man box allow violence against women, girls and other marginalized groups to persist."

"A Call to Men asks men to step out of the man box," Porter told a Minnesota reporter in 2017, "to release themselves from these rigid notions of manhood . . . and be your authentic self."[4] By dividing masculinity into positive and negative—healthy or toxic, in the box or out of it—gender analysts like these imply that only negative masculinity is a performance, whereas the positive version expresses what is real. Positing a self that floats outside culture, race, socialization, and worldly power structures, these critics naturalize masculinity even while they expose it as a product of culture.

### Convo: What about White, Cisgender, Straight Men?

**Erica:** I'm not unhappy that #MeToo is making some individual men have to be more cautious in their actions. Who holds all the power? It's mostly old white guys. Men and people in power positions. I don't feel like there is any epidemic of false accusations, or that so many "good" men are being attacked, et cetera. We know women very rarely falsely accuse men of sexual assault. And in my spheres, I don't really see any men losing power, resources, positions. There's some huffing and puffing, but the house is staying fairly secure. If these guys are second-guessing their behavior, good.

**Judith:** I'm not saying there are a lot of false accusations—or that women are "crying rape." I'm saying, let's be careful, because it makes a difference to the credibility and the effectiveness and ethics of a movement, and also to people and relationships. I also want to be sure that we don't forget that given the right circumstances, a lot of different kinds of people can do sexual harm. Not just white cisgender straight men. My ultimate goal is a different, more expansive sexual culture. I don't want a paranoid sexual culture. I'd rather that women be able to say no, and for that to be the end of it. That doesn't preclude people in power knowing what's too much or responding correctly when harm is done.

## Potential Alliances: Intersectional Feminist Men

We support progressive men's anti-violence work in helping men to interrogate their self-conceptions and attitudes, change their behavior, and intervene when they see other men acting in misogynist or violent ways. But the efforts we admire most are those that take the next, necessary, step: applying an intersectional analysis of structural oppressions, and challenging men, no matter how marginalized or hurt they may be, to recognize their own privileges and to accept the leadership of women and queer men in transforming not just themselves but the world.

**Erica:** Isn't a "paranoid sexual culture" a matter of perspective, though? There really has never been an equitable sexual culture, whatever that is. When institutions try to regulate or police sex, it's always going to be the most vulnerable who will be caught up. I know so many queer people who have been hauled up on all kinds of sexual harassment charges at universities for making heterosexual students uncomfortable. But the cisgender white men who prey on students seem to sail along.

I am not interested in any rhetoric that elevates the value of a "culture of flirting," or whatever people call it. In my work/life experience, that language is patriarchal, heterosexist—it centers the people already at home and secure in public space. I am not nostalgic or interested in valorizing that. I'm not sure there was a "good old days."

**Judith**: I'm not nostalgic. I'm just heterosexual! I don't want to perpetuate the power and privilege of cisgender, straight white men either, but I also have sympathy for them. I believe they have to change and can change, but not through shame and blame. We've talked about the imaginary: going beyond the language and structures we have to envision worlds that are entirely different. I'm not dreaming back to the 1950s; I don't want to live like *Mad Men*. Can we imagine a sexual cultural where people get to have their sex lives, safely and freely?

At CONNECT, working on the principle of "men and women as allies in preventing and ending all forms of violence," the organization's codirectors have long experience in counseling and activism, and in working at the intersections of violence, race, class, and gender inequality. Quentin "Q" Wolcott, a middle-aged Black man, roots his work in marginalized communities. MacNichol, a white woman in her sixties, is an ordained interfaith minister.

"A lot of men who are doing some sort of masculinity or empowerment work are lacking in terms of analysis," says Wolcott, in a conversation with MacNichol and Judith at their office in a Harlem public school repurposed as a hub for community organizing. CONNECT, which works almost entirely with men of color and poor white men, constructs the analysis from the ground up, bringing together racism and sexism. "We use parallels: where are the places you feel hopeless, powerless?" he continues. "You feel this way under this system. Imagine your partner, your wife, your girlfriend, your children under this system. For many of them it's like 'Oh wow, I get it now! I'm replicating my powerlessness within my family.'"

While working in solidarity with others in the men's anti-violence movement, MacNichol and Wolcott have been struck by the absence of another critical piece of the work: accountability. "We went to a healthy masculinity conference a while back," MacNichol recalls. "I was so freaked out. I think they used the word 'sexism' once in a workshop. I'm big for healing and looking at your own wounds, but I never got the feeling that people were holding those two things together—one's own woundedness from socialization and the real consequences for women and other men."

Other smaller and more fluid networks, like New York's Challenging Male Supremacy Project, California's Oakland Men's Project, and Chicago's Circles and Ciphers also try to organize men to unlearn violence. Influenced by transformative justice, these groups are creating "spaces and developing tools for working with men and masculine-identified people to challenge male supremacist practices and cultures as part of a broader movement for collective liberation," as Alan Greig, cofounder of Challenging Male Supremacy, described its work in a 2016 blog post.[5] With few to no paid staff and a focus on personal, political, and local transformation through workshops, circles, and storytelling, these groups have strong parallels to 1970s-era feminist consciousness raising. Compared with the impact of the latter and its offshoots on hundreds of thousands of everyday women, however, these men's groups are a drop in the bucket. Perhaps this speaks to the urgency of women's liberation, which galvanized hundreds of thousands of women almost instantly. Voluntary relinquishment of male power is a harder sell.

Still, these activists understand that it has to happen, and that it is only by linking the interpersonal and the systemic that we will undo both kinds of violence. "You could live in a patriarchal society and never put a hand on someone, but the fact is that you have all these other benefits," says Wolcott. Like whiteness and white supremacy, "male privilege is invisible, misogynistic attitudes are invisible. Patriarchy is not just a spot on the page. It's a whole page."

## Beyond Gender

We support men's organizations and movements that are engaged in radical, anti-racist, and pro-feminist work to prevent interpersonal violence and dismantle the structures that breed and sustain it. But there's one more thing these men (and all of us) have to do if we're going to beat gender violence: fracture, reimagine, recombine, destabilize, and demote gender so radically that it ceases to have any fixed meaning. And if we can't throw out the whole taxonomy, we can at least we shake its legitimacy. While agender, genderfluid, and nonbinary individuals and organizations are building movements that advance these options—in 2017, for instance, Oregon allowed video game designer Patch to legally identify as agender, that is, neither M nor F—most cisgender men engaged in what might be called the mainstream men's anti-violence movement have concluded that this is too far a stretch.

We get it. They first need to induce other men to recognize that gender exists, before asking them to imagine undoing it. Nevertheless, we have a hard time distinguishing the kind, compassionate, honest, upstanding creature that sociologist Michael Kimmel calls a "good man" from a good person, regardless of the genitals attached. Similarly, sexually obnoxious, exploitative power wielding (the characteristics of Kimmel's not-so-good "real man") is not a behavior exclusive to men. Many women, including queers, benefit from and reinforce patriarchy. Ending sexual violence will require unpacking the hidden privileges and costs of gender and redressing its harms. And since all oppressions are interrelated, this work must be done in tandem with the dismantling of other systems of domination like white supremacy and ableism.

The end of gender would not end coercive sex, but if sexual violence is an exercise of power—and gender is one of the most powerful of power hierarchies—then moving beyond gender would also go a long way toward creating egalitarian and inclusive relationships, families, and communities, where everyone gets to be their "authentic self."

# 11

# Women Against the Regime

"What is your relationship to feminism?" Judith asks Vicki Henry, head of Women Against Registry, or WAR.

Her reply: "I hate it."

It is a sentiment that, in our experience, is not uncommon among the members of WAR, a small group launched in 2007 at the first national conference of the organization Reform Sex Offense Laws. The convention was convened with the aim of pulling together the fledgling grassroots mutual aid and advocacy groups of registrants and their supporters that had sprung up around the country. Henry, the mother of a Marine convicted of child pornography possession, had proven herself as an able leader in Missouri. So RSOL organizer Paul Shannon asked her to head up a national women's subgroup of RSOL. "There was a need for "a place where wives, daughters, girlfriends would have an outlet for their anger and energy," says Shannon, now chair of the renamed National Association for Rational Sex Offense Laws (NARSOL). Henry accepted eagerly.

Tactical and personal differences have since divided Henry and Shannon, and she has taken WAR independent. But there is one thing on which the two agree: feminism. Like most of the registered citizens and their friends we have met, both perceive feminists as political insiders, almost as responsible for the SO's plight as the state is. "Part of the reason we are where we are is because the feminist movement created this, and now it's got this landslide effect," says Henry. Shannon concurs: WAR was conceived "to oppose the feminist assault on sex offenders," he says.

We have talked about feminists' part, significant though not dominant, in the buildup of the sex offense legal regime. But what about the role of women in the SO movement and their relationship to feminism, victims' rights organizations, and survivors themselves? That role and that relationship are surprising and complex. For while there are many men in both the leadership and the rank and file—and of course, the objects of the laws are almost all men—the registrants' rights movement is a women's movement.

## Mothers' Crusades

In much criminal justice reform activism, women—specifically, white mothers—are the instigators, the spokespeople, and the foot soldiers. So it has been with the sex offense legal regime. In the 1970s, women were instrumental in founding the victims' rights movement, which provided the jurisprudential assumptions on which the sex offense legal regime rests, with organizations including Families and Friends of Missing Persons (1974), Parents of Murdered Children (1978), and Mothers Against Drunk Driving, or MADD (1980).[1] After Etan Patz's disappearance in 1979, his mother Julie lobbied for the establishment of a national clearinghouse of missing children, which was established in 1984 as the National Center for Missing and Exploited Children. To this day, NCMEC's fear-inducing statistics continue to ratify the creation of more and more "child protective" sex laws.

Patty Wetterling—mother of eleven-year-old Jacob, snatched and murdered in 1989 in St. Joseph, Minnesota, while riding his bike—lobbied for sex offender registries, first in her state and then nationally, resulting in the federal Jacob Wetterling Act of 1994. While still an advocate for missing children—she is chair of NCMEC—Wetterling has become one of the most vocal opponents of sex offender registries, arguing that they ruin lives while failing to protect children. Around the same time as Wetterling was pressing for registries, Ida Ballasiotes and Helen Harlow—Washington State mothers, respectively, of a young woman raped and killed by a man out on work release, and of a seven-year-old boy raped, mutilated, and killed by a paroled repeat assaulter—organized Friends of Diane and the Tennis Shoe Brigade. Concerted agitation by these two groups impelled state elected officials to enact the nation's first "sexually violent predator" law, permitting indefinite civil confinement. After seven-year-old Megan Kanka was kidnapped from her home, raped, and killed in suburban New Jersey in 1994, her mother Maureen fought to expand the registry to include community notification of sex offenders' release from prison. That led to federal legislation requiring the same. All of these people are working or middle class and white.

Just as mothers, and white motherhood—that spotless badge of devotion and courage—played a significant role in the institution and extension of registries and community notification laws, white women are also proving instrumental in the move to challenge the registries. The sex offense legal regime was built in the name of protecting children. Similarly, these women's ferocity in fighting the regime rises in their children's defense.

Women run most of the state organizations; the current executive director of NARSOL is a woman, Brenda Jones, although leadership of the national organization is heavily male. These women gain valuable political experience—in public speaking, lobbying, organization-building—as they advocate for their sons and husbands and challenge this facet of the prison nation. They are public figures and community leaders.

Yet in their hearts and public presentation, just like their counterparts in the victim's rights movement, they are always mothers. Thanks to the difficulty of finding work or housing, and forming or maintaining romantic relationships and families, men on the registry often end up in their childhood bedrooms. As well as their sons' advocates, these women, not always willingly, become their breadwinners, housekeepers, and companions. And recently, many states have added a fiendish new mandate that in order for a person with a sex offense to return home, a member of the household must pay to be trained as a chaperone. The minder is usually the mother. Conscripted into doing the state's policing labor, she must accompany her son, brother, or partner wherever a child may be present, and report him to law enforcement if he violates parole or probation.

### *"Voice of the families"*

Tonia Maloney founded Illinois Voices for Reform when her nineteen-year-old son was convicted of criminal sexual abuse and child pornography for his relationship with his sixteen-year-old girlfriend. On an early, now removed, website for the organization Maloney described the actions for which he is now on the registry as "his indiscretions." Mary Sue Molnar of Texas Voices was mobilized to action when her then-twenty-two-year-old son, as she put it, "made some really bad choices" and was convicted of a sex offense for a relationship with a sixteen-year-old female. "I think that every parent, especially those with sons, should be deeply concerned about the current laws, because their sons could be on the registry in the blink of an eye," she said on a local TV report.[2]

While the figure at the center of the case is often silent—the young men rarely make public comments or appearances—these mothers animate campaigns that portray their white heterosexual sons as youthful and foolish, engaged in normal sexual play. In the view of these women, the real problem is a state that too heavily punishes innocent men and boys. The government, they reason, should not be intruding in the private lives of people who are not harming anyone.

Henry rarely speaks publicly about her son. In fact, while WAR's energy and image are maternal, it established itself as "the voice of the families"—"the innocent women and children being destroyed by public registration": children whose fathers are not allowed to attend a school football game, families rendered destitute, kids shunned at school—the "collateral damage" of sex offense laws. The group also expresses concern for the child victims of abuse, and stresses, in its opposition to the registry and residency restrictions, that such policies do not protect children.[3]

Gender creates an optic essential to the organization's effectiveness. When Women Against Registry arrives with a banner bearing its name, people are curious and surprised. But equally strategic is avoiding public expressions of sympathy for the bad guys. "We don't say, 'Oh, those poor sex offenders.' We say, 'Hey, they did wrong, they've been penalized, they don't need to be punished for life and neither does their family,' " Henry explains.

Among those attracted to the movement, however, are also women whose family loyalties are torn and who cannot take an unequivocal stance in favor of the registrant. "Terri," approaching Judith at a NARSOL conference, blinks back tears and pushes her sharply cut blonde hair behind one ear as she describes the anguish of being caught in the middle. The accused abuser was her teenage nephew, the accuser her five-year-old niece. Some in the extended family blamed the children's mother, Terri's sister, for what happened. Terri feels for them all. "We can love the sinner, even if we hate the sin," she says. But that injunction does not mitigate her pain: "Both these children are on my heart." So why is she at this meeting? She believes the laws, including prohibitions on contact between the brother and sister, are preventing the family from healing.

## *Unheard*

In portraying their boys as victims of the system and the families as collateral damage, this movement, sometimes unwittingly, pushes one person to the periphery of the circle of sympathy: the person who experienced harm. Speaking in 2015 about a high-profile case of a nineteen-year-old boy accused of assaulting a fourteen-year-old girl, Jones of NARSOL said: "In a court of law, the burden is on the accuser. And in this case, at that point, it is the fourteen-year-old. We try to put the person who's crying rape on this little pedestal and not allow them to testify. But that is putting an unnecessary burden [on the defendant]. You're supposed to be innocent until proven guilty."[4] This is an important statement about the presumption of innocence and the constitutional rights of criminal defendants. But here, the survivor is depicted as the guilty party—the one "crying rape," perched on a "little pedestal," coddled by the state. There's no acknowledgment that both parties need protection.

Asked whether she sees any similarities between herself and feminists, Vicki Henry answers that she's for equal pay and doesn't want men to treat women "as property." She wants women and men to be equal. But equality, she suggests, means equal responsibility. "Women should respect men, and men should respect women. If people had respect for themselves and for others and thought about that, it might help with some of the situations we see and the things that happen."

What "situations and things?" Judith asks. Henry expands: "This is very controversial. I'm talking about guys that get in trouble at a college party and both the males and females are drinking. If you had respect for yourself, I don't think you would drink in excess. I think about guys the same way."

Some feminists have expressed misgivings about the excesses of student anti-violence feminism. Judith has written, for instance, that it is not "rape denial" to advise young women (and men) to avoid getting so drunk that they cannot take care of themselves. But Henry's and the SO movement's common description of the problem minimizes or omits what is front and center for feminist anti-violence movements of all politics: rape is real and too prevalent, and it can still be rape even if the woman acts "irresponsibly."

## *Critical contributions*

Women like Henry, Jones, and Molnar have achieved national and statewide visibility for issues facing people with sex offense convictions, particularly by challenging the placement of juveniles on sex offender registries. They have educated countless policymakers and law enforcers, prevented passage of bad laws, kept their members up to date on political and legal developments, and provided support for a severely demoralized group of people. Their work is crucial and commendable, and it falls within a long tradition of women's activism.

Yet rendered invisible by these organizations are central insights gleaned over centuries of feminist organizing: many men *do* harm the children and the women in their lives. Belief systems such as patriarchy and white supremacy naturalize or minimize this violence. Men and boys may be foolish, rebellious, and make "bad choices," but it is equally true that children and women are groped, assaulted, and raped.

## Carceral Feminism Redux: From Pornography to "Trafficking"

Because sexual violence is about sex and power, a feminist response to sexual violence depends on how a movement conceives the relationship between sex and power. Thus, over the last thirty years, intertwined with the conflict between carceral and anti-carceral feminisms have been a series of ideological and tactical skirmishes over what constitutes sexual exploitation, and how women and other vulnerable groups can be protected from it.

The latest struggle is over sex work. It divides roughly between "prostitution abolitionists," who view all sex work, whether coerced or voluntary, as "sex trafficking," exploitative and criminal; and the sex worker rights movement, which views sex work as a job whose difficulties are connected to unfair labor practices, migration, health care, and myriad social and economic inequalities. This latter group opposes policing and criminalization as threats to workers' safety and livelihoods.

But before the movement against "sex trafficking," which emerged in the 1990s, were the "porn wars" of the 1980s.

### *The porn wars*

To the perplexity and dismay of many feminists, the fight against porn—and the subsequent counterattack against that fight—absorbed much of the energy of the white anti-violence movement for nearly a decade. The proximate issue was a local anti-pornography ordinance, written by feminist legal theorist Catharine A. MacKinnon and writer Andrea Dworkin, that was introduced in 1983 in two Midwestern cities. The law defined pornography as "the graphic sexually explicit subordination of women through pictures and/or words"—not as speech, but as an act of violence—and allowed women to sue pornographers for sex discrimination.

Enacted in Indianapolis, the law was promptly challenged and overturned as a violation of the First Amendment. Nevertheless, the war on porn established the ideas that would animate the next carceral feminist crusade: "prostitution abolitionism." It also moved middle-class, white carceral feminists further from the struggles of poor women and many women of color.

While the anti-porn movement was pouring its energy into banning sexually explicit images as the cause and instrument of violence against women, other anti-violence feminists, largely women of color, were allying with prisoners' rights advocates, death penalty opponents, and some communist and socialist organizations to fight against the criminalization of women of color who killed their rapists and abusers in self-defense. These included women like Joan Little, sentenced to death for the 1975 killing of a white deputy sheriff who tried to rape her in a Beaufort, North Carolina, jail; and Bernadette Powell, a Black woman in Ithaca, New York, facing fifteen years to life for the murder of her husband, who had relentlessly abused her for six years.[5]

And while anti-porn activists leapt onto their white horses to rescue damsels who were not in distress, such as exotic dancers and adult film actors, their "pro-sex feminist" opponents—queers, sex radicals, members of marginalized erotic communities, and civil libertarians—warned that similar crusades against sexual immorality had historically restricted the freedoms of their intended beneficiaries and eclipsed actual, corporeal violence against women. For example, in response to a spectral epidemic of forced prostitution of young white women, the Woman's Christian Temperance Union and other white do-gooder women's groups campaigned for passage of the White Slave Traffic Act, or the Mann Act, of 1910. Meanwhile, white racist vigilantes, abetted by Jim Crow laws, were carrying out a war of lynching and terrorism against formerly enslaved Black Americans, a principle tactic of which was the rape of African American women and girls.

### *"Sex trafficking"*

When the pro-sex forces won the porn wars, the antis did not raise a white flag and retreat. The crusade against pornography had psyched the Reagan administration and conservative Christians, titillated the press, and mobilized US lawmakers of both parties to crack down on sexual commerce. Now, joined by other carceral-leaning feminists engaged in work against domestic violence and rape, anti-porn feminists took their sharpened ideologies and tactics to a new field of battle.

To stir wider anger—and attain more influence—they took the crusade against prostitution global, linking it to the horror of human trafficking, which includes labor exploitation of all sorts. They called it "sex trafficking," painting lurid pictures of shady operators recruiting women for legitimate jobs in other countries, taking their money to get them over the borders, and then selling them into sex slavery. The new campaign produced rhetoric that would prove invaluable to law-and-order and immigration hawks. For instance, the Trump administration separates minors arriving at the US–Mexico border from the adults they are traveling with on the pretext that these adults may be child sex traffickers posing as relatives or guardians. But the word "trafficking" serves multiple purposes: among them, it also resonates with labor rights activists concerned about abuses in the mobile global economy.

### *A tale of two migrants*

By 2013, reporting on two undocumented immigrants in the news in Vermont, Judith observed how this logic and rhetoric had come to dominate public perceptions of sex work and law enforcement policies toward it. Danilo Lopez, from Mexico, worked on a dairy farm and was an organizer for the grassroots group Migrant Justice. "Rose" was a Korean masseuse at a spa that sometimes offered a "happy ending," a hand job to finish off the services. The week after an "exposé" in a local paper, police raided Rose's workplace, several similar establishments closed, and Rose disappeared.

Rose told the reporter of that story (he gave her the pseudonym) that she was on duty day and night, seven days a week; she was paid only in tips, and lived on the premises. The one place in the area she could identify was the Macy's where she bought cosmetics. The reporter noted covered windows, surveillance cameras, and a lack of visible cash registers. His sources called these features "red flags" that the workers were being held captive.

According to organizing materials from Migrant Justice, Vermont's Mexican farm workers "typically labor 60 to 80 hours per week and endure extreme isolation, often without a clear sense of where they are." They exist in "highly restrictive living and labor environments, and are overly dependent on employers to meet their basic needs," unable to "gather as a community, go to the hospital, or go to the market."

Yet in spite of these comparable situations, public perceptions of migrants like Danilo and Rose cannot be more different. The male farmworker is seen either as a hard-working "good immigrant" or as a job-snatching criminal. In either case, he is understood to be in the United States of his own volition. By contrast, police, media, and prostitution abolitionists construe an Asian woman in a situation like Rose's as the docile, guileless victim of trafficking—because surely no one would come to the Land of Opportunity to give hand jobs. His exploitation is seen as economic; hers is moral. He needs political organizing (or deportation); she needs rescue.

It is more the rule than the exception that migrants work twelve, eighteen, or (in the case of live-in domestics and caregivers) twenty-four hours a day. But what holds them in their jobs is not usually an evil captor. Rather, it is the immensely unequal global economy. Faced with washing floors at less than minimum wage, or pleasuring penises at a tips-only average of twenty dollars an hour (or three times the minimum wage), Rose's decision makes sense. How did she get to the United States? Did she pay a human trafficker who promised her a different, better job? We don't know.

The language of trafficking "has become a way to talk about the internationalized aspects of things that have been happening for a long time—kidnapping, forced labor, lying to someone about being hired when they are actually being entrapped in a bondage scheme—as if they were one distinct phenomenon," gender and sexuality scholar Svati Shah told Judith. But in common parlance and the shorthand of immigration officials, "'trafficking' basically means prostitution"—including the voluntary kind.[6] Shah has written: "Without addressing the contexts of livelihood and migration, the conditions that make sexual commerce a viable livelihood strategy for poor people around the world continue to exist."[7]

## *"Trafficking" comes home*

Aside from influencing international law enforcement and immigration policies, as well as the discourse in many global women's rights communities, carceral anti-prostitution activists have made important legal inroads in the United States. In 2017, they claimed that Backpage.com, a hookup site frequented primarily by gay men, was allowing traffickers to advertise underage girls for sexual services, identifiable by code words such as "Amber Alert." Facing possible legal action, Backpage eliminated its commercial sex ads, from which it had derived almost all its revenue. Other sites, such as Craigslist, followed suit. The federal government undertook an investigation of Backpage, and in 2018 it seized and shut down the site. Soon thereafter, Congress passed the Allow States and Victims to Fight Online Sex Trafficking / Stop Enabling Sex Traffickers Acts (FOSTA-SESTA), which make it easier for individuals to sue and law enforcement to shutter websites they say are abetting trafficking by accepting sex ads.[8] In the panic to sanitize their sites, Internet platforms also took down legal sex educational tools and resources.

In cracking down on such hookup sites, advocates and authorities construct the pimp, or "trafficker," not as the abettor or collaborator with the worker in breaking the law, but as the perpetrator of interpersonal violence against the worker, his victim. To end and prevent this violence, the pimp must be prosecuted and punished. Other prostitution abolitionists take this a step further, aiming to reduce not just the supply of commercial sex but also to discourage the demand. To do both, several Northern European countries have enacted laws based on the "end demand"—or Nordic—model of prostitution control, in which pimps and clients are arrested, and workers are induced to quit the profession and inform on the "traffickers."

In the United States, prostitution abolitionists have not generally pressed for the Nordic model. They have, however, urged the stepped-up use of federal anti-racketeering statutes and the Mann Act (which criminalizes transportation of persons across state lines for the purposes of illicit sexual activity) to prosecute both "traffickers" and clients,[9] as well as placing johns on the sex offender registry as a means of deterring other would-be johns.[10] The National Conference of State Legislatures' bill tracking database shows that in 2017 alone, more than a dozen states and the District of Columbia passed laws under the heading of sex trafficking that criminalize new aspects of prostitution, lengthen statutes of limitation, or increase penalties.[11]

### *Unintended consequences*

These laws are more likely to harm voluntary adult sex workers than to safeguard exploited women or children. Sex worker organizations say that FOSTA-SESTA robs them of independence, income, and safety by driving their work underground and onto the street, and blocking channels through which workers promote safety by swapping information and blacklisting abusive clients. The law has a cascading effect, according to Erica Friscioni, a core organizer with Support Ho(s)e, who also leads campaigns to support sex workers who are in jail or facing stiff sentences for defending themselves against violent clients. "The more financially destitute or in need a worker is, the more likely they are to be pushed into unsafe, riskier situations, sometimes ignoring their gut because they need to make rent and survive," says Friscioni. Journalist and former sex worker Melissa Gira Grant calls the online platforms "a form of harm reduction."[12] Moreover, because such platforms are global, workers everywhere will feel the effects of FOSTA-SESTA.

After France adopted the Nordic model in 2016, Médecins du Monde (Doctors of the World) surveyed nearly 600 sex workers and organizers about the new law. Most respondents said the new law "had a detrimental effect on [their] safety, health and overall living conditions." Thirty-eight percent said it disempowered them, making it harder, for instance, to demand that clients wear condoms—with the shift of legal risk, men felt they had more prerogative to set the terms. In all, 88 percent of the workers opposed the criminalization of clients.[13]

### LGBTQ Youth and Survival Sex

- A 2012 Williams Institute Study found that 40 percent of homeless youth identify as LGBTQ.[14]
- In 2015, the Urban Institute surveyed 283 LGBTQ youth who were homeless and/or engaged in survival sex. An overwhelming number said they were driven from home by families or faith institutions that vilified them for their sexuality or gender identities and/or subjected them to physical, emotional, and sexual abuse.
- Many of the youth reported denial of services by public housing, shelters, food banks, and clinics.
- 90 percent were nonwhite, and nearly 20 percent identified as transgender or gender-expansive.[15]

Anti-trafficking enforcement also has unintended consequences for the "children" it purports to protect. For one thing, most of the young people who trade sex for money or food are not children; they are adolescents. A disproportionate number of them are LGBTQ, driven to the streets by intense transphobia and homophobia at home or school. The police do not see these youth, particularly if they are of color, as children in need; they see them as delinquents and criminals.

Wes Ware, a Louisiana LGBTQ youth worker and former director of the New Orleans queer and trans youth of color organization BreakOUT!, says that trading sex to survive often ensnares young people in the criminal legal system and puts them at risk of the immediate and lifetime consequences of being labeled a sexual predator or sex offender. "Imagine you are seventeen and you and your sixteen-year-old friend are out and both of you are trading or selling sex for survival. You use the buddy system because that's the safest thing to do, to not be alone," says Ware. "But if both of you are caught by the police, depending on the state, the seventeen-year-old could end up charged with trafficking a minor for sex." In some states, that's enough to land you on the sex offender registry.

## Sex Workers Organize

The logic of trafficking forecloses the possibility that a sex worker can make choices, and it severs that choice from the larger economic and social conditions that favor sex work over other means of making a living. As long as an occupation is defined as degradation and exploitation—something for which no rational person would volunteer—someone who chooses to do it must be either crazy, deeply traumatized, or coerced. The sex worker can be recognized as a rational agent only when she relinquishes her claim to agency and agrees to be construed as helpless.

Many sex workers fervently reject this characterization of themselves and are rising up against the hyper-policing and criminalization of their occupations. Among them, the now-shuttered Chicago-based Young Women's Empowerment Project (YWEP)—an organization led primarily by youth of color with the mantra "We are not the problem, we are the solution"—organized against the rescue narrative; it was one of the earliest groups in the United States to raise the alarm about how anti-trafficking legislation would dramatically harm domestic sex workers—particularly the most marginalized, including young people. YWEP built multiple ways to support sex workers, including needle/syringe exchanges and access to free health care, sexual health education, food, and technology. It also published a number of groundbreaking reports that sharply critique the carceral state's response to sex work, including "Girls Do What They Have to Do to Survive" (2011), chronicling resilience and tools for survival, and the "Bad Encounter Line: How Youth in the Sex Trade and Street Economy Are Turned Away from Systems Meant to Help Us and What We Are Doing to Fight Back" (2012).[16]

Across the globe, in grassroots groups from Bay Area Workers Support in California to the Massachusetts Sex Worker Ally Network, from Australia's Scarlet Alliance to India's Sampada Grameen Mahila Sanstha, organized sex workers are demanding *rights, not rescue*. Increasingly, sex workers current and former are writing articles and books reclaiming their own narratives and promoting policies that would enable them to ply their trade without danger, malevolent interference from the government, or unwanted rescue from charities.[17]

Like the French workers in the Médecins du Monde survey, these people stress that criminalization endangers them in the same ways that FOSTA-SESTA does. They are also knocking down the pedestal on which certain "supporters" have placed them. Indeed, in the 1980s, "pro-sex" feminists (including Judith) romanticized sex work as sexually and personally empowering. For some women it is; for others it is not. But increasingly, sex workers are expressing fatigue with being batted between pity and idealization, and losing interest in the debate over whether they are victims or victors.

They have boiled the situation down to this: Sex work is work. People do it because it pays the bills, offering more money and flexibility than many other jobs. The message from these organizers is that no task of work is inherently dignifying or degrading. Empowerment comes with the protection and promotion of a person's rights as a worker, a global or national citizen, and a human being—her rights to bodily integrity, self-determination, and collective action.

## Potential Alliances

### *Sex workers and "sex offenders" unite*

There is little hope that prostitution abolitionists and sex worker organizers will find common ground, so antagonistic are their worldviews. But two other constituencies that seem almost as far apart—if not ideologically, then politically and socially—have allied in their mutual defense against state crackdowns on their lives and livelihoods. While police have long tossed people in jail for exchanging sex for money, politicized sex workers have kept their distance from other "sex offenders." Nor have organizations largely made up of middle-class gay men made common cause with those working in the street-based sex industry. Both these positions changed in Louisiana in 2010, when these two groups both faced becoming registered sex offenders for the same "crimes."

For decades, in addition to the illegal act of prostitution, street sex workers in New Orleans were charged with "solicitation of a crime against nature" (SCAN), a felony prohibiting "unnatural copulation"—that is, oral or anal sex. The Supreme Court's decriminalization of sodomy in 2003 did not change that: the ruling referred only to behavior in private. After that decision, Orleans Parish and other Louisiana jurisdictions made SCAN a sex offense, which meant listing on the public sex offender registry and the imposition of other restrictions and penalties, including the printing of "sex offender" on your driver's license. As in other gentrifying cities, these laws had little to do with public safety and everything to do with "cleaning up" the streets for chic new shops and restaurants, and for wealthier, usually white, homeowners.

Jordan Flaherty, reporting on the story for *Colorlines* and other grassroots news outlets, found that after the hardened SCAN statute, more than half of people on the public sex offender registry in Orleans Parish had been convicted of offering anal or oral sex for money. Of those with SCAN convictions, almost all were women, and 78 percent were African American. But the statute also threatened white, middle-class gay men.

To fight back, the New Orleans sex worker rights organization Women with a Vision built a coalition called NO Justice, uniting sex workers, anti-violence organizations, prison-industrial-complex abolitionists and reformers, LGBTQ people, and civil rights advocates to challenge a statute that threatened both street-based sex workers and people who cruise for consensual sex around bars or in public parks or toilets.

The NO Justice campaign demanded fundamental social change, not rescue. "Society needs a war on the systems that facilitate poverty, not a war on impoverished women," its policy brief read. "Helping society's most marginalized women to succeed is a better strategy to improve public safety as opposed to further alienating them away from society."

In 2011, NO Justice won a lawsuit in federal court, and the statutes were repealed.[18]

The campaign demonstrated that it is possible to repeal bad laws and stop attempts to expand the registry by building broad-based coalitions and educating allies. Most important, this campaign showed the strength of a strategy that centers the leadership and experience of some of the most marginalized folks in our communities—in this case, street-based sex workers of color. The NO Justice campaign did not moralize or devalue sex work; it did not demonize public or casual gay sex. Instead, it showed how the criminalization of consensual sex harms people, particularly women and queers.

### *Abolition: A meeting point*

Unfortunately, the New Orleans campaign did not demand an end to the sex offender registry. Nor did it directly and clearly state that public registries make no one safer. But the victory of workers at the bottom rungs of the sex industry—who are arguably as abased as "sex offenders" are reviled—in building broad, multiracial, cross-class solidarity gives hope to those working toward the goal of bringing together people of widely different classes, races, and life situations to abolish the sex offense legal regime.

Among these alliances might be one between the (currently anti-feminist) women of the SO rights movement and abolition feminists. The obstacles are not trivial. The two movements are at best unaware of each other, at worst mutually hostile. SOs are unlikely to have heard of abolition feminists, and for good reason: mainstream carceral feminism takes up most of the space in the media and legislative circles. Then again, few abolition feminists have opened their arms to people convicted of sex offenses either.

But it is not essential that Vicki Henry or Brenda Jones call themselves feminists. There is a more straightforward path: abolition feminists and the women of the SO movement can come together over *abolition*, of both the sex offense legal regime and the carceral state. In fact, WAR already calls itself "an organization dedicated to the abolition of the sex offender registry"—a position into which it evolved, and which is more radical than the movement's at large. It is no great leap to recognize the destruction the punitive state delivers upon everyone in its clutches, with women carrying a heavy burden.

The first overture may need to come from feminists like the two of us, who want to forge connections—at least to reassure SO mothers that we are not all gunning for their sons. The next steps are harder, and in the end may come to naught: conversations about the ways that racialized and heteronormative gender roles—particularly masculinity, whether individual, cultural, or governmental—trap both their sons and their daughters in cycles of violence.

# 12

# Restorative and Transformative Justice: Making the Road

> *"Wanderer, your footsteps are the road, and nothing more; wanderer, there is no road, the road is made by walking."*
>
> Antonio Machado
>
> *Plains of Castilla*, 1912

In feminist law firms, student unions, and legislative committee rooms, carceral feminists and victims' rights advocates continue to press for more policing, longer sentences, and more extensive restrictions after prison (although a few victims' advocates now criticize the registries, mostly because their harshness may inhibit victims from reporting abuse by relatives or other adults they are close to). In unions and workplaces, male anti-violence workers are trying to change other men's hearts and minds. In church basements and the locked dayrooms of civil commitment facilities, people convicted of sex offenses are fighting for their rights. Each of these groups is attacking some part of some problem, with varying degrees of success. Some are working with the state to respond to what the state defines as crime. Some are working to change the consciousness of individuals who have done gender-based interpersonal harm or might do so in the future. Some are trying to reform or abolish the regime the state has built to correct and "manage" people labeled as sex offenders.

But as more people recognize that the US punitive state is doing more harm than good, if it does any good at all, the term "restorative justice" seems to be everywhere in the air. This is particularly so as the #MeToo movement ponders what's next. Do we just lock men up or "cancel" them forever? Or is there a way forward that would demand accountability and facilitate healing, while changing our communities and culture so as to prevent more harm in the future?

Restorative justice, or restorative practice, is a set of principles and methodologies for addressing and redressing wrongdoing. These practices have been in use in industrialized countries worldwide since the 1970s but are adapted from much older, indigenous forms of justice—the Maori traditions of Aotearoa, or what is called New Zealand; the "peacemaking circles" of the North American Navajo and other North American Native ways of dealing with transgressions of community law or mores; the Gacaca courts, originating in precolonial tribal Rwandese justice practices, a version of which was instituted after the mass atrocities of 1994; and others.[1]

Whereas the criminal legal process is a formalized contest between the "people"—that is, the state, represented by the prosecutor—and the "defendant," represented by a lawyer, with the harmed person often sidelined, restorative justice brings "crime" back to the relationships among the harm-doer, the people directly affected, and the community. The criminal system seeks retribution, while restorative justice seeks accountability and repair; it guards against adding more harm to harm already done. RJ gives priority to the harmed person's needs, yet it does not require that anyone judge others or take one side, either with the "perpetrator" or the "victim." Acknowledging that all of us have done harm and all have been harmed at some time in our lives, RJ aims to bring everyone into the circle as a moral equal.

For some people, especially in marginalized communities, RJ does not go far enough, because it fails to contend with—or work to change—the contexts in which violence is condoned and perpetrated. Indeed, critics contend that those doing RJ within the oppressive institutions of the criminal legal system may be unwittingly collaborating with it. This understanding—plus the experience of communities for whom the state is often not a benign, much less protective or helpful, actor—is the wellspring of transformative justice, which came to life around the turn of the twenty-first century.

Transformative justice is closely related to the principles and practices of restorative justice, but there are also essential differences between the two. A short working definition of TJ is RJ plus political organizing. Like RJ, TJ is not new, but builds on informal networks of conflict adjudication, protection, and care, particularly among people such as precariously housed transgender people, sex workers, and street youth—that is, those who are likely to see the state as an antagonist, not a friend. Like its predecessors, transformative justice practitioners not only eschew reliance on state systems of policing, investigation, prosecution, and punishment; they also recognize those systems as part of the problem, as forces that alienate individuals and communities from their agency and perpetrate violence against them.

But TJ practitioners also know that individuals and communities want safety, so they work to provide it through webs of mutual aid and responsibility, teaching each other necessary skills, such as first aid in neighborhoods where the police do not respond in time to save a shooting victim. When some of these practices are adopted by communities and constitute part of longer-term community-building efforts—and when they intentionally exclude the participation of any state actor or institution—they may be called "community accountability."

## Restorative Practices

Even among folks committed to the abolition of the prison nation, there are some who feel it is important to bring the values and practices of restorative justice into the systems and institutions with which people interact every day, such as the courts and public schools, colleges and workplaces.

### *The criminal legal system*

Restorative justice is increasingly lodged within the criminal legal system, and it is used with both workers inside the courts and "corrections" system, and those under its control. According to *Stateline*, as of 2016 thirty-five states had adopted legislation encouraging RJ for youth and adults either before or after detention or prison; in other places, even without legislation, law enforcement departments refer certain cases to nonprofits that implement RJ.[2]

RESTORE: Responsibility and Equity for Sexual Transgressions Offering a Restorative Experience, based in Arizona, is a collaboration among law enforcement, public health agencies, sexual assault services, and prosecutors that seeks to "facilitate a victim-centered, community driven resolution of selected individual sex crimes that creates and carries out a plan for accountability, healing, and public safety."[3] Vermont's Department of Corrections maintains a network of community justice centers, where volunteers engage in restorative practices with people at different stages of the criminal legal process—to forestall an indictment, replace incarceration, or aid reentry. At any given time, there are as many as forty circles of support and accountability (COSAs) operating in the state.

New York City's Center for Court Innovation is partnering with the city's judiciary to institute restorative practices within the system. One of its most vibrant outposts is the Red Hook Community Justice Center, in a gentrifying Brooklyn neighborhood that is still largely Black and poor, with a few white working-class families left over from the days when it was a working port. The judge at the RHCJC sends the vast majority of cases for resolution in the peacemaking circles, and increasingly area residents request the circles' help in working through conflicts with neighbors or family members, such as noise, vandalism, or disrespectful interactions—before they reach the point of violence or arrest. And in California, the Ahimsa Collective employs its restorative and peacemaking approach to interpersonal and sexual violence in many programs throughout the state's department of corrections and rehabilitation.

### *Repairing schools*

Public schools, as well, are beginning to benefit from the introduction of restorative practices; in some places, school disciplinary procedures of detention, suspension, or expulsion are being replaced with circles of communication, accountability, and repair. Rather than being "reformist" simply by virtue of location, some of the school-based practitioners have a long radical lineage. For instance, Morningside Center in New York was founded in 1982 under the name Educators for Social Responsibility. ESR's vision of a future without war and hatred led its organizers to collaborate with schools from kindergarten through high school, where they taught students peacemaking and peer mediation skills. Over the years, Morningside has matured with the field, and now brings social and emotional learning and restorative practices to schools nationwide. It is working with the New York City public school system to establish several model all-restorative schools.

### *Title IX*

Restorative justice is also gaining popularity on campus as a way to respond to sexual harm, thanks in part to disappointing results of the current, adversarial Title IX procedures, and those of earlier disciplinary processes. This is no fringe movement. The American Bar Association's 2017 Task Force on College Due Process Rights and Victim Protections recommended it.[4] Early adopters included the University of Vermont and Skidmore College, and in the past two years, numerous other institutions of higher learning, including the Universities of Colorado, Michigan, and Kentucky, Stanford University, and Brown University, have implemented RJ programs; in some cases they've folded these into the offices enforcing federal Title IX regulations. So far, assessments are positive. Almost 100 percent of students who accessed the University of Colorado RJ program reported satisfaction on a variety of measures. For instance, they said they felt "safe," "treated like a person and not a criminal," and glad that "the focus was on community education and relations and not punishment or shaming."[5]

## Transformative Justice

TJ emerged in relation to restorative justice, so it employs many of the same methods and shares its basic principles. But for many practitioners with an abolitionist stance, doing RJ inside state-run systems is too compromised. Among their misgivings: the courts represent participation in RJ-based "alternative" programs as voluntary for both the survivor and the "responsible party." But how voluntary can these be, when the other "option" is indictment or jail time? How complicit are these projects with the punitive systems they're lodged in?

Aside from questionable uses by the state, RJ is also amenable to corporate scams. Walmart hired the ominously named Corrective Education Company (CEC) to provide "restorative justice for retail theft." CEC's clients can offer people they identify as shoplifters an alternative to a call to the police: a coerced payment of $400 and six hours of online "behavior therapy." A San Francisco judge deemed this practice "a private, pseudo-justice system that is based on profit" and "textbook extortion," and banned CEC from operating in California.[6]

Most important, TJ was born in communities that have never been able to rely on the police for safety—Black people living under Jim Crow, undocumented immigrants, street youth hustling sex to survive. TJ's innovations have their origins in practices that evolved in these communities to ensure mutual protection and deal with interpersonal harm. TJ, therefore, is community based from start to finish, abjuring cooperation with police, courts, and corrections departments altogether and working instead to dismantle the carceral state, which wastes millions of lives, fractures families, and decimates neighborhoods.

But even while TJ's critique of the *punitive* state is deep and thoroughgoing, its practitioners are not aiming to replace what should properly be government functions, such as the provision of good housing, schools, parks, streetlights, childcare, health care, and the redistribution of wealth through fair taxation (or some other economic system altogether). TJ is not one of what George H.W. Bush called "a thousand points of light"—charities that were supposed to step in when the state sloughed off its obligation to ensure the wellbeing of people and communities. Transformative justice is a replacement for policing and caging, which have failed to diminish gendered and sexual violence or care for its survivors. As Shira Hassan, cofounder of the TJ capacity-building collaborative JUST Practice (JP), told Erica, "The state has been failing survivors since there have been survivors."

Since 2000, networks and organizations that are invested in building transformative justice have proliferated. Some call their practice "community accountability," because the term stresses ways in which communities—friend circles, church groups, neighborhoods, workplaces—collaborate to advance the goals of TJ.

Some of these groups were inspired by Generation Five, an organization born in 2000 with the thrillingly immodest mission of ending child sexual abuse in five generations—without criminalization. Many were sparked into being by the 2001 "Statement on Gender Violence and the Prison Industrial Complex," released by Critical Resistance and INCITE!. "We call social justice movements to develop strategies and analysis that address both state *and* interpersonal violence, particularly violence against women," the statement began. Such responses must "not depend on a sexist, racist, classist, and homophobic criminal justice system"; they must "also provide safety for survivors of sexual and domestic violence. To live violence-free lives, we must develop holistic strategies for addressing violence that speak to the intersection of all forms of oppression."[7]

Self-identified survivors around the globe continue to create and support other visionary TJ groups, often in response to their own experiences with the criminal legal system. There's Sista II Sista (New York), Creative Interventions and the Storytelling and Organizing Project (Oakland), Philly Stands Up (Philadelphia), Young Women's Empowerment Project (Chicago), the Audre Lorde Project's Safe OUTside the System (New York), Communities Against Rape and Abuse (Seattle), Undercurrents (Melbourne), TJ Kollectiv (Berlin), and possibly hundreds of others. Below are some whose innovations have been replicated elsewhere, or are just widely admired.

### *Storytelling and Organizing Project*

STOP, initiated in Oakland, California, in 2004 as a project of the anti-violence organization Creative Interventions, gathers stories from "everyday" people—survivors, friends or family, bystanders, and the occasional person who perpetrated harm—about the ways they responded without calling the police. To facilitate free and open discussion, the audio and transcripts are posted on the website without comment.

In one narrative, Maria finds out after many years that her former boyfriend, a corrections officer, sexually abused her daughter. Believing it's too late to call the police, she creates her own form of public accountability:

> I took his picture, and I remember putting . . . a warning sign with his picture on it and writing on there something like, "A Warning—Beware of child sexual abuser. Unable to prosecute due to statute of limitations." And I made sure it was posted from his house all the way to where he needed to take his train and where his community needed to take the train. There were hundreds of them.

Maria also learns that her brother was a perpetrator:

> And I confronted him with it. I told . . . my other siblings who also live in California with him about it, and then I told him I needed to talk to him about it. And I told him, I says, you know, "My daughter says you did this, this, this, this, and this, and I believe her" . . . There wasn't much response verbally or otherwise except that he was quiet. His wife was at this meeting. She was there. But there wasn't any denying.[8]

Naming harm within Maria's family was a step toward exposing sexual violence in a place where it is often hidden. But her solutions also reveal the possible mistakes, or opportunities for questioning and learning, that TJ and community accountability groups contend with.

On its own, will exposing the harm-doer change things? By posting flyers in the perpetrator's neighborhood, Maria is "informing" the community. But is her low-tech public shaming any better than the state's sex offender registry? Where does information end and revenge start? Maria leaves it to the neighbors to act. Where does demanding accountability become vigilantism?

Do Maria's actions honor the bedrock principle of restorative and transformative justice: to respond to harm without doing more harm? And, as an unpaid, self-styled one-person safety team, Maria is accountable only to herself. Is that what we want? How will those responses rise beyond reaction to transformation? TJ rejects stock answers, but groups like STOP proliferate stories that people can learn from in generating their own, local ideas for ensuring safety and accountability and repairing the effects of harm.

## *Liberated Ground*

For many TJ practitioners, a first goal is to learn how to solve problems without calling the police, a move that can cause a cascade of harm and trauma—arrest, jail, court dates, deportation, prison, and the loss of jobs, housing, and even of children, who may be wrenched away to foster care or adoption.

Starting in the late 1990s, Brooklyn-based Sista II Sista (SIIS) built a successful neighborhood campaign, through "many years of street outreach and conversations," to make their neighborhood safer for young women by reducing gender-based harassment in their neighborhood—including by the police. The group planted flags—that is, they posted flyers—marking "Sistas Liberated Ground," a "harassment-free zone," and they set up a hotline for women to call to strategize responses to violence without policing. After September 11, 2001, as surveillance increased in many communities, SIIS organized know-your-rights trainings and self-defense workshops, all pushed by "day-to-day organizing work, such as door knocking and flyering." SIIS "went from getting bottles thrown at our doors by young men who didn't understand the need for a women's space to gathering hundreds of neighborhood supporters—who were multigenerational and not just female—at street actions against the police and military."[9]

### BYP100: A Transformative Process—in Public

In 2015, Malcolm, a high-profile young male member of the Chicago chapter of Black Youth Project 100 (BYP100) was accused of sexual assault by Kyra, in detailed posts on Facebook and Medium. BYP100, which focuses on "transformative leadership development," direct action, advocacy, and education, is explicitly anti-carceral, and its leadership is feminist, Black and queer. BYP100 believed Kyra, and put in place a process to address the harm. According to Mariame Kaba, who helped facilitate the process, Kyra "never wanted him exiled from the community. She wanted him to take accountability for the harm he caused her."[10] Among survivors of sexual assault, this is a common, if not universal, response.

Malcolm was placed on hiatus. A support team for Kyra was formed, and an accountability team for Malcolm. Participants set goals and structures within which they could be accomplished. From Kyra's public statement to the final circle—which included both Kyra and Malcolm—the process took over fifteen months and required the unpaid labor of many people, particularly Black women. Local media chronicled the incident and the organization's subsequent moves. To balance confidentiality with the need and desire to inform and politicize a wider community—and quell rumors—the group posted updates on Tumblr.

Kyra's needs were heard and validated. Malcolm was not shunned or stigmatized, yet he took responsibility for his actions. "I am accountable to the communities I serve and strive to continue making amends to Kyra," he stated publicly.[11] BYP100 prevented one young Black person from entering the criminal legal system, and multiple communities learned about sexual assault, consent, harm—and achieving accountability without engaging the criminal legal system. Preventatively, the group is working on an "enthusiastic-consent curriculum." While imperfect, all of this unfolded without handcuffs, courts, or prisons.

### *Pod Maps*

The Bay Area Transformative Justice Collective, which emerged in 2013 to focus specifically on building TJ responses to child sexual abuse, has seen its Pod Map project take off. The map, conceived to make the "imaginary notion of community concrete," is a worksheet of concentric circles. The survivor puts herself in the middle and then fills in the surrounding circles with individuals, groups, or community organizations, in decreasing levels of closeness and trust, on whom she can draw for varied forms of support—for instance, to help with healing or hold a person accountable. But Pod Maps have been adapted for a wide range of uses—to help make safety plans for individuals experiencing interpersonal violence, or to visualize the reach of a nonprofit organization or collective by mapping all the participants' support systems.[12]

### *Safety Labs*

San Francisco's Community United Against Violence (CUAV) for years organized "safety labs" and a "safetyfest" in which participants used "real-life scenarios and practical skills to help us intervene in, prevent, and heal from harm without creating more harm." The neighbors are still partying and it's 3 a.m. A friend is trying to leave an abusive partner. What do you do before and after a crisis to ease in-the-moment tension or violence and prevent actions taken in anger, fear, or confusion? The safety labs remind participants that they are not alone, even if they feel that way.[13]

### Convo: Whose Job Is Change?

**Judith:** I interviewed a Black woman—I'll call her Angela—who runs a community justice center in Vermont and does RJ every day. But she won't have anything to do with sex offenders, because she was badly abused as a child. I asked her, "How could I persuade you that sex offenders also must be justly and fairly treated?" She said, "What do you got?" I went through a few arguments, and some made sense to her. But she still didn't want to work with SOs.

**Erica:** I get where Angela is coming from. And the work is not to persuade her. I am appreciative of her willingness to support RJ practices and to interrupt silences. The stigma, the silence, the shame—there's a whole architecture we have invested in that is a tool of heteropatriarchy. Shame and stigma have worked against feminists and ending sexual violence. It is part of ending the harm to name and dismantle that architecture.

**Judith**: I don't really think this is true—that there is silence around sex and abuse. I'm more with Foucault and [cultural critic] Jim Kincaid on this—that we can't stop talking about it.

**Erica**: It's asymmetrical. "We" as a culture can't stop talking about "it" and its varied proxies, but I am not at all sure individual people who have experienced sexualized gender violence feel this same sense of freedom and openness to talk about their experiences.

**Judith:** Or to do something like RJ. "I believe in restorative justice—except for my rapist." Totally understandable.

**Erica:** Angela doesn't have to be the one to deal with the SOs. Just like the work to challenge white supremacy does not have to be

### *Social media*

The news, and the skills, of TJ are spreading on the Internet and social media—zines, Instagram, Facebook, and Tumbir. Among resources available online are *Ten Things to Do instead of Calling* done by every person of color or every POC organization. So for someone who has experienced sexual violence, maybe it's not their frontline collective action to be working for fairness for SOs. They've got lots of stuff to do already!

A person who has been harmed can decide they don't want to call the cops on the harmer, and support and invest in the value of a TJ process. But maybe they personally don't have the bandwidth to run or organize or even participate in that process. Part of the framework of community accountability or TJ processes is to acknowledge that a wider group of people are involved in individual acts of harm, and we need more: more people naming the problem, acknowledging that trouble exists, working to challenge and interrupt learning and behaviors, and working with people who have done harm. The individual can't do all the work alone.

**Judith:** This is an important point. It's up to the harm-doers to take accountability, and it's up to others who have not been traumatized to confront those who do harm, work sympathetically with them—whatever it takes. That said, it's moving and powerful to hear victims of sexual violence come out for sex offender rights. In fact, Angela also said as much. She believes SOs deserve rights. She believes that they're redeemable—that everyone is redeemable. She just cannot personally face these guys. She feels too angry.

**Erica:** That she is willing to say, essentially, "not in my name" is really important. This chips away at the idea of "victim rights" as uniformly in support of more punishment. In fact, one of my responses to someone who is upset and angry is to say "I am fucking angry too!"

*the Police; Five Ways to Help Someone in a Mental Health Emergency without Calling the Police; Abolish the Police—Instead, Let's Have Full Social, Economic, and Political Equality*; and others. There's even an app called *Bouy*—"Call a friend, not the cops"—to support people in building mutual aid.

## "Slow Work"

Like most grassroots organizing, and like any movement that is inventing itself as it goes along, TJ groups may live precariously. Some reject the idea of TJ as paid labor and eschew both the professionalization and the foundation grant funding that have distanced other movements—reproductive rights, environmental justice—from the lives and priorities of the people who have the most at stake. Yet with scant money, staff, or permanent space, such formations must contend with burnout and turnover. Projects pop up to address a problem and then drop off the map, without having mustered the wherewithal to document their practices. But what documentation this movement, now several decades old, has produced offers much instruction and inspiration. For instance, while Generation Five has been on hiatus since 2017, before taking the break it assembled its considerable cache of tools, exercises, and experiences in a sixty-eight-page opus, *Ending Child Sexual Abuse: A Transformative Justice Handbook*, which it posted online for anyone to use.[14]

No one involved in transformative justice or community accountability—or any restorative practice, for that matter—believes that change will be fast or easy. This is what anti-poverty lawyer Dean Spade calls "slow work." Messy work. Transformation is a process of trial and error, of breaking down what went wrong and using that knowledge to improve the next initiative, like turning a failed crop into compost and plowing it back into the soil. And as Shira Hassan cautions, "It is impossible to do this work without mistakes." But TJ groups, she notes, can create "generous and generative" spaces for people to listen, "reflect on what they would have done differently, and to sit with that—how do they want to shape their practice?"

Restorative practices are used by the carceral state, but they are not the property of the state. They are flexible forms, available to practitioners of transformative justice, community accountability, and all their variants. Participation in restorative or reparative processes, moreover, is consciousness raising. Along with witnessing—if they have not directly experienced—the injuries of gendered sexual violence or criminalization, people who participate in RJ circles can take what they learn back to their homes, workplaces, and organizations.

But the accomplishments of RJ will be limited if it does not broaden its scope to radically remake the environments in which it operates. For instance, to diminish sexual harassment and assault on campus, colleges and universities need structural changes, such as education that instills a critical stance toward oppression and inequalities of race, sex, gender, and ability; fair pay for graduate students and all campus workers; and the elimination of near-medieval hierarchies of privilege and indebtedness that characterize academe.

Our task here is twofold: to infuse our organizing with restorative and reparative values and practices; and, in turn, to politicize restorative practices. The embodiment of that politicization is transformative justice: changing not just ourselves and each other, but also our world.

# PART IV

# Ten Ways to Confront Sexual Harm, End State Violence, and Transform Our Communities

1. Abolish the Sex Offender Registry and Civil Commitment
2. Demedicalize Sexual Violence
3. Decriminalize Child and Teen Sexuality
4. Invest in Radical and Free Sex Education
5. Complicate Consent
6. Eroticize Safety, Proliferate Pleasures
7. Build and Sustain a Robust Welfare State, Not a Carceral State
8. Think Intersectionally
9. Practice Transformative and Restorative Justice
10. Embrace Abolition Feminism

## *Reform or Radical Change?*

It is easy to dismiss many of the projects and organizing efforts we've described in this book as random, improvisational, or—that damning word—utopian. Where is the evidence of their success? What are the metrics? Skeptics sigh sympathetically, smile condescendingly, and deliver the verdict: yes, the current system has its flaws, but, alas, *there is no alternative*. So often is this argument voiced that it has an acronym, TINA.

If TINA is true, we have to treat the criminal legal system like an old car. We need transportation. The car is basically sound, but it has a few broken parts. So we should fix the brakes, get a new muffler. Then it will be fine. "There have always been prisons." *Maybe we just need more reasonable prison sentences.* "To protect the public, we must keep track of 'sex offenders.' " *How about a "smarter" sex offender registry, with only the "right people" on it?*

TINA masks the reality that the prison industrial complex is not broken. In fact, it is working precisely as designed—to exact vengeance, warehouse those left behind by late capitalism, perpetuate white supremacy, and make money, to name just a few of its functions. Far from progressive, small corrections to the criminal system are akin to "tweaking Armageddon," as abolitionist and geographer Ruth Wilson Gilmore offered at a 2004 California convening on movement building called "The Revolution Will Not Be Funded: Beyond the Nonprofit Industrial Complex."[1]

Should we reform the systems and institutions we have? Or must we go for radical—root-level—systems change?

We can do both—carefully.

Rather than conceive of reform and radical change as opposites, it's useful to see them in a relationship of both cooperation and tension. We are not against reform. Rather, we believe in practice propelled by vision. So like other abolitionists, we ask the question: Does this reform move us toward or away from the goal of the campaign or project, and ultimately the vision of the movement of which it is part? Reforms that liberate more people, delegitimize the carceral regime, or make material differences in the lives of people under its control are what the French Marxist André Gorz called, in 1964, "non-reformist reforms."[2]

Throughout this book, we have offered examples of many kinds of organizing and activism. Some of these efforts are reformist without a radical vision—they even reject such visions as embarrassingly impractical. Others, however, use non-reformist reforms as tactics in a strategy to achieve profound transformation.

We envision a world where there are no more registries, no more prisons. We want an end to gender and sexual violence because that opens safe space for creativity, connection, and meaning—not to mention good sex, whatever that means for the people doing it. In the final section of this book, we sketch that vision, or some of it, along with some ways to achieve it. None of the ideas proposed here are blanket solutions. We don't believe those exist. Neither is any of them a top-down change or an overnight conversion. We can almost guarantee that they won't happen smoothly. Change requires collective thought and action, so we expect conflict. We, and the people whose work we applaud, are in it for the long haul, so we expect periodic fatigue. And because organizing works simultaneously on many fronts, we tolerate, in fact kind of relish, messiness.

We invite you to argue or agree with these ideas, love or leave them, fill in the blanks, and build other possibilities.

# 1

# Abolish the Sex Offender Registry and Civil Commitment

## The System Cannot Be Fixed

The body of law known as Sex Offender Registration and Notification (SORN)—including the myriad state and local requirements of registration, as well as restrictions on residency, work, travel, association, and simply being—is a legacy of the moral panics of the 1980s.

Civil commitment is prison, without the sentence or release date. It is preventive detention—being locked up for crimes you might commit—the freedom from which was one of the first-ever civil liberties and is now globally recognized as a human right. A quarter century ago, some politicians came up with the diagnosis of the "sexually violent predator" to legitimize this preventive detention. Today, a gulag of prisons masquerading as mental health facilities stretches across the nation. Its "patients" are considered incurable, so most will never get out.

The sex offense legal regime does no good and much harm. It displaces real child protection with a false sense of security at the same time as it incites terror to justify itself. Like the rest of the criminal legal system, it disproportionately targets people of color. It exiles a permanent class of sexual pariahs—now nearly a million—from the rights of residency, citizenship, and humanity itself.

It is long past time to overthrow the regime.

Legal challenges, brought largely by the registrants' movement and their allies, are beginning to chip away at aspects of the registry. But because the registry is an edifice built on emotions—revulsion, terror, sentimentality—we will never dismantle it without changing people's minds *and* hearts. Those emotions might eventually change on their own, once a critical mass of Americans know and love someone on the registry, just as a critical number of people have been directly touched by the prison industrial complex. But like mass incarceration, the longer we wait to get rid of SORN and SVP laws, the greater and less reversible their harms will become.

To assuage the fears of marauding pedophiles and "predators" that keep this regime alive, it is not only necessary to unpack and repudiate the racialized, punitive, sex-phobic, and anti-feminist culture those emotions spring from. In place of paranoia, we need to nourish queerly anti-racist cultures of gender equity, and a celebration of erotic joy in all its variation.

# 2

# Demedicalize Sexual Violence

## Foster Social Approaches to Harm and Healing

Since the courts have largely resisted attempts to declare civil commitment of "sexually violent predators" a criminal, punitive measure, a tempting response would be to take the state's word for it—to treat these prisons as hospitals, and work with disability rights activists to ensure that the residents are guaranteed the same protections as other people with mental health challenges under the Americans with Disabilities Act and other related laws. The ADA sets stringent criteria for nonconsensual psychiatric commitment, including due process and frequent evaluations of whether a person may remain in detention.

But there's a problem with such an approach, no matter how adversarial: it keeps people with sex-related convictions in the hands of the agencies and individuals that construct "sex offending" as a psychological disorder, and that have a vested interest in convincing the rest of us that only they can treat it.

Usually with the best of intentions, these professionals derive their livelihoods and reputations from running the in-prison sex offender programs and civil commitment facilities; psychologically "managing" people on the registry; performing and interpreting risk assessments; giving expert testimony in sentencing and civil commitment hearings; conjuring new sexual disorders; and training, speaking, and publishing about all of the above. In the view of this crowd, sex-offense-specific treatment—"evidence based," of course—is the solution, not the problem. We do not expect them to start entertaining existential questions, such as *Is what I do every day useful?* Or, *Should I find another line of work?*

People who commit sexual harm have commonly experienced trauma as children or adults. Like most of us at some point in our lives, they could use therapy. But civil commitment is prison, and incarceration is psychologically destructive; indefinite detention borders on psychological torture—the opposite of therapy. Furthermore, the "treatment" arm of the sex offense legal regime asks us all to collaborate, recruiting the public, helping professions, schools, religious institutions, and even families to police the state's boundaries between sexual normalcy and deviance.

The radical approach to civil commitment is to stop thinking of sexual violence as a psychopathology from which the community must be safeguarded, and to instead turn to social and environmental approaches that engage the community in helping people who have done harm to live nonviolent lives. These include restorative practices like circles of support and accountability (COSAs), as well as the varying processes of community accountability being created and refined within a context of social justice.

We speak of these practices as forms of help, but a better description would be "mutual aid." For while volunteers sustain COSAs and other such practices, we chafe at the framework of volunteerism, whose implication is that the core member is the beneficiary of altruism. We need to support one another not because we have a cause, as Dean Spade writes, but because we seek "a life focused on our commitments to radical transformation."[1]

# 3

# Decriminalize Child and Teen Sexuality

## Recognize the Vulnerability and Support the Self-Determination of Youth

Age of consent establishes a single, uniform threshold in time, the day before which a person is considered sexually and emotionally ignorant and the day after which we expect her to know everything. That person is also innocent the day before and—should the sexual partner still be on the "minor" side of the line—criminally guilty the day after. The laws make no accommodation for normative child and teen sex play, individual differences in degrees of maturity, or cultural variation. The consequences of breaking the laws, even without knowing you are doing so, can be devastating and lifelong. And as we've seen, punishment is widely variable depending on race, class, gender, and sexuality.

We need both to enable young people to explore their sexuality and also provide avenues through which they can come forward if an adult is sexually harming them—without fear that they will trigger the most extreme responses, such as child custody investigations or criminal prosecution. For twelve years, the Netherlands managed to do both. From 1990 to 2002, Dutch law made sexual intercourse legal for people ages twelve to sixteen, including with people above the legal age of majority. If a young person felt she was being coerced or exploited, however, she could bring a complaint to the child protective agency. Only in certain cases could a parent or the government challenge a young person's judgment that she was consensually engaging in sex. "Overall, the legal message here [was] that children over the age of twelve are sexual and potentially self-determining, and they remain weaker than adults, and should be protected accordingly, but not under the autonomous authority of parents," wrote Scottish sociologist

David T. Evans in *Sexual Citizenship*.[1] Importantly, these were matters for human services, not the criminal legal system.

In 2002, the Dutch succumbed to the same pressure that led to the expanding criminalization of sex in the United States and established a hard age of consent at sixteen, violation of which can be penalized by prison and/or fines. There is a close-in-age exception.

New Orleans LGBTQ youth organizer Wes Ware recognizes that age of consent laws contribute to criminalization of youth—particularly queer and trans youth whose sexuality is already framed as deviant—and to the policing and prosecutorial practices that use the laws to deny youth both agency and protection. But mainstream adult LGBTQ organizations tend to shy away from challenging these laws. Ware urges moving toward a vision rooted in a culture of radical sexual consent, while ensuring that youth have access to the things that will increase agency and safety: education, housing, employment, health care, public transportation. Of course, the danger in these strategies is that the main issue—age of consent statutes—remains neutral, invisible, and legitimized.

We must never abandon children to endure or defend themselves when they are subjected to sexual harm. But the United States abandons children in countless ways—leaving them without decent housing, health care, clean water, playgrounds, and so much else. Singling out sex as the one thing to worry about reflects adult anxieties more than it does a concern for children's well-being. The criminalization of consensual child and teen sex does not protect; it harms.

# 4

# Invest in Radical and Free Sex Education

## Not Just "Skills," but Ethics, Too

Rather than cloister children and teens to protect them from gender violence and sexual harm, we need to give them the freedom to love their bodies, and help them learn to communicate about relationships, pleasures, and personal boundaries. Their genders and sexualities need to be affirmed, their prejudices challenged. They need practical information, such as the necessity of HIV testing and the legality of abortion. Most of all, they need to be nurtured as ethical, caring human beings.

In a country where most states don't even require education about contraception, good luck getting any of the above in school. As for sexual desire or pleasure, in most public school classrooms, the only way it enters the conversation is if the students bring it up—and it is the rare skilled, courageous, and, you could say, sneaky educator who will speak frankly about what is, after all, the reason most people have sex. Parents are reluctant to talk to their kids about sex, and after a certain age a lot of kids don't want to hear it from them. Faith organizations, with the notable exception of the Unitarian Universalists, don't do it. So where does a curious young person learn about sex?

The same place they learn about, and do, everything else: online.

We're not talking about pornography, although, for better or worse, that is a source of sex education, as are friends, books, and TV. The good news is that the Internet is a rich source of accurate, sex-positive info.

### *YouTube and lube*

Sex, Etc., staffed "by teens for teens," has been around for decades, providing "unfettered access to comprehensive sexuality education," as well as opportunities for activism to promote sexual and reproductive rights and justice for youth. Advocates for Youth's AMAZE produces videos—mostly animations aimed at middle schoolers—that tend toward cutesy at one end and merciless at the other. (Big sister to little: "If either of you are high or drinking, you cannot consent, period.") In any case, they are popular: in less than four years the YouTube channel has garnered over 33 million views and 141,000 subscribers.

Planned Parenthood's frequently updated library of videos explores topics ranging from how to know if someone wants to have sex with you (or not) to what to expect when you use the morning-after pill. The videos are short, sensitive, and even sexy. The actors come in all races and the couples in every gender combination. Too bad they're also uniformly slender, young, and conventional looking in every way. No gender-nonconforming folks here—or even a pimple.

One of the liveliest, most pleasure-positive, funny—and feminist—sources of sexuality information in any medium is Scarleteen.com. The independent site—whose tagline is "Sex ed for the real world"—turned twenty in 2018. The staff, led by founder Heather Corinna, describes itself as "queer, working class and woman-led." The tone is accurate but not academic, ethically unswerving yet un-preachy.

The site's archive of thousands of articles, as well as forum posts from tens of thousands of users, contains entries on subjects from first kisses to fisting to fatphobia. Asexuality ("ace" is in the glossary) is presented as a choice as fine as any. There is also plenty on consent—defining it, recognizing it, negotiating it. But Scarleteen is also political on the subject. In one blog post, Corinna stresses that good sex ed prevents rape by helping young people discover "what mutually wanted, shared pleasure can look and feel like." Good sex ed prevents gender violence by excluding "gender or sexual roles or stereotypes that enable and perpetuate rape/sexual abuse, [and] suggests learners strongly question them." And "good sex ed recognizes [that] everyone with the right to say no also has the right to say yes; that only empowering no isn't very empowering at all."

DIY sexpertise, once a loss leader of adult stars selling paid content on their sites, is now as abundant on YouTube as instructions on how to mend a torn screen door or remove pop-ups from your computer screen. The sexperts come in every size, color, and dis/ability. There's Laci Green, a thirtyish white woman with a low décolletage, huge glasses, the ability to sound perky about herpes, and almost 1.5 million followers. Along with such subjects as cuckolding and yoni eggs, she dedicates videos to abortion rights and gets into the weeds (in two installments) of feminist debates on gender. The lusciously large African American host of "Glamerotica101," Tyomi Morgan, can be seen in black bodysuit and red, white, and blue thigh-highs straddling a male assistant and demonstrating "How to Ride: Basic Moves" ("Tuck and roll your booty, and bounce your booty"). And a video in which able-bodied assistants help two white German lovers with severe muscular dystrophy to touch, kiss, and use sex toys has been widely posted by disability rights sites.

### *An "ethic of mutuality"*

Even when they're diverse and sex positive, most sex educators share one shortcoming: they are teaching *skills*—how to prevent HIV transmission, ride a lover, or say no. All this misses the point, says Sharon Lamb, a family psychologist and professor. Sexual relations, like all other human relations, exist in a moral universe, and they all exist in the same moral universe. From this realization, Lamb and her graduate students have developed curricula, one for middle schoolers, one for college students, that reframe education about sexual relationships from consent-versus-assault to an emphasis on "mutuality and reciprocity." This is not "skills training," says Lamb. It's an ongoing process of figuring out how to live.

Ethical thinking can be nurtured in small children, who develop a fierce sense of fairness early on and are eager to engage in discussions of big philosophical questions. It is relevant to adolescents negotiating complex situations and issues, from friendship cliques to responses to gun violence and the racialized violence of policing. A "sexual ethic of mutuality" is a balance of self-protection and altruism; it means bringing your most thoughtful, attentive, and generous self to sex, whether it is casual or committed. Such an ethic is also political: it represents a resistance to the every-person-for-themself doctrine of neoliberalism. It is an intrinsically feminist concept, at the heart of building a world in which communities look out for the vulnerable and all persons are valued for who they are.

# 5

# Complicate Consent

## Move beyond "Yes Means Yes"

In 1991, a student group called Womyn of Antioch devised a new definition of consent, and their college released a guide based on it: in any sexual encounter, partners had to express, verbally, their desire to engage—not just at the start but with each new kiss, caress, or insertion. Without this, the guidelines suggested, the whole business could be rape. The Antioch rules, as they came to be known, were ridiculed, but the idea of affirmative consent—yes means yes—took hold. By 2014, 800 campuses had adopted it as a standard for adjudicating sexual assault in Title IX investigations.[1] Today, in feminist parlance and progressive sex education, a clearly communicated (though not necessarily verbal) "yes" is the criterion for whether a sexual act is wanted or unwanted, and therefore licit or illicit.

We like the idea of "yes means yes"—who wouldn't?—but as, say, the name of a feminist adult film production company, not a legal standard.

That's because affirmative consent reproduces what psychology professor Charlene Muehlenhard and Zoe D. Peterson, director of the Kinsey Institute's Sexual Assault Research Initiative, call the dominant—problematic—"dichotomous model" of consent, which leaves out a lot of sexual territory. "Many people, including the public and researchers, treat sex as either wanted or unwanted, with wanted sex being consensual and unwanted sex being nonconsensual," they wrote in a 2007 article for the *Journal of Sex Research*. "Real life, however, is often more complicated."

In a study Muehlenhard and Peterson conducted, women undergraduates revealed many permutations of want and consent: some had consented to unwanted sex—to please a partner or strengthen a relationship. Some wanted sex but did not consent—say, because they feared pregnancy. One wrote of wanting and not wanting sex at the same time: she felt turned on but guilty about having sex before marriage. In other words, many sexual situations are ambiguous.[2]

We are not saying that consent is always relative or debatable, or that there is no such thing as sexual abuse or assault. Nor are we suggesting that children and young adults do not need help learning how to express their needs and desires and understand their partner's, whether that person is saying yes, no, or maybe. But if, as Muehlenhard and Peterson demonstrate, "yes means yes" hardly covers all the bases, how might we refashion consent more broadly?

Luckily, there are people who have thought a great deal about consent. Those who engage in BDSM (bondage-discipline / sadism-masochism) intensify their arousal by playing with the malleable categories of wanting and not wanting. In BDSM, weeping, shouting "no," or pleading for the dominator to stop does not mean "stop"; being pushed beyond one's limits, or pushing someone beyond theirs, is the turn-on. So BDSM practitioners become adept at expressing their desires and needs, and at being sensitive to those of their partners. Prior to sex, the players talk about what is or is not okay, and to mitigate confusion, agree on a "safe word" by which the bottom (the masochist or person being disciplined) indicates that she *really* means stop. A top who does not honor the safe word is not welcome in the BDSM community.

Like the BDSM and kink communities, sex workers regard explicit communication concerning consent as a critical part of doing business, but they also maintain other personal criteria for what kind of sex they have, and with whom. Consider sex-worker organizer Erica Friscioni's clear-eyed description:

> "I understand consent, in my work, as what I agree to offer in exchange for money. Activities that I would not engage in unless paid to do I have no problem engaging with if I am being properly compensated. Economic consent is done through verbal or written consent between myself and the client. Obviously we all have limits

> and boundaries, and there are some activities I will not perform for any amount of money. However, there are activities I enjoy engaging with for no compensation because they are personal and private, differentiated from my work and economic consent.

Friscioni suggests that there are two categories of sex in her life—the transactional and the relational. The contract between a businessperson and her client is not the same as the intimate exchange between lovers. The requirement of affirmative consent brings the transactional into a space that aspires to be experimental, forgiving, and free of quid pro quo.

If "Be considerate and don't do things another person doesn't want you to do" is kindergarten "sex" education, then getting familiar with sex toys or BDSM—or any of the infinite permutations of fantasy and touch, attraction, relationship, or commerce—might be considered adult continuing sex education. Negotiation of the ambiguities of wanting and not wanting, consenting and not consenting, giving pleasure and asking for it, is part of that ongoing education.

# 6

# Eroticize Safety, Proliferate Pleasures

## End Violence to Make Space for Connection

"I am certain that pleasure is the missing piece in our movement(s) for a new world," wrote adrienne maree brown—organizer, doula, author of *Emergent Strategies: Shaping Change, Changing Worlds*, and self-described "pleasure activist"—on her blog in 2010. Brown's commitment to pleasure activism stemmed from her own experience with sexual assault in high school, and her recognition that she was likely not "the only human who started their sexual life on the defensive." For brown, pleasure is a pathway to mitigate risk, to build cultures, and to practice safer sex.[1]

We can trace brown's pleasure politics to, among other times and places, the 1980s, at the terrifying debut of the AIDS epidemic. While gay men sickened and died, the Reagan administration moralized and dithered; by 1987, when the Food and Drug Administration approved the first treatment for HIV, 50,000 Americans had been infected and all but about 2,000 had perished.[2] Rather than attacking the pathogen by investing in prevention, treatments, and cures, the government—with the support of religious and political conservatives, including some gay men—attacked gay people. The pretext was public health, and the target was the polymorphous, communal sexual cultures that exploded in the cities after the 1969 rebellion at New York's Stonewall Inn.

In 1984, and again ten years later, the government deployed emergency health codes the way vice squads had used liquor licensing laws for decades: to raid and shutter queer bars, clubs, and bathhouses, a task they performed with special viciousness against Black, brown, and working-class gays, lesbians, transfolks, and drag queens.

The irony—and tragedy—of the crackdowns was that the practices that drastically reduced infections and deaths, at least in white, middle-class gay communities, were born and propagated in the bathhouses. Even before the epidemic, the baths were considered safer than public parks or toilets, where men risked assault, robbery, and police harassment. Now, recognizing that the community had to save itself, lovers became comrades and invented safer sex, eroticizing condom use and other transmission-preventing practices.

"Gay men's experimentation with a wide variety of sexual pleasures and shared sexual ideals has been a crucial factor in our ability to adapt to the necessities of safer sex during the AIDS epidemic," wrote the late art critic Douglas Crimp in Sex Panic!, an eponymous pamphlet produced by the direct action group in 1997. "We trusted each other, we changed our experimentation to incorporate safer pleasures, and we saved untold numbers of lives."[3] In the same publication, Jim Eigo, an early organizer with the Aids Coalition to Unleash Power (ACT UP), noted the "unspoken taboo against anal sex without condoms" at the baths and a "communal inducement" to practice safe sex.[4]

This commitment to the protection of bodies and erotic communities in the face of oppression helped forge the politics and relationships, in many different communities, that have sustained resistance to attacks both persistent and new, whether that means the ongoing violence of policing against trans sex workers or the criminalization of HIV transmission.

The most recent cadres of pleasure activists, many of them queer and/or feminist survivors of sexual and gender violence, carry the conviction that sexual liberation is not the enemy of safety. They also embody the promise that sexual trauma does not condemn a person to perpetual sexual pain; experiencing harm is not the end of the road.

Ignacio G. Rivera, a sex worker, queer indie porn producer, and survivor of child sexual abuse, is a fellow of Just Beginnings—a "movement-building platform designed to initiate, cultivate, and fund strategic efforts to end child sexual abuse."[5] The message of Rivera's numerous talks, podcasts, and workshops: cultivate sex positivity. For instance, Rivera's (Re)Nude* Sex(uality) initiative supports sexuality education, particularly for "survivors of child sexual abuse and sexual trauma in finding/continuing their sexual health/liberation journey."[6]

While Rivera, brown, and Just Beginnings create conversations about pleasure that begin with people who have experienced harm, others use pleasure to resist a different kind of violation: the slander that their bodies are the problem. Sins Invalid, a collective of people with disabilities, gives performances, including one called "Crip Sex Moments" and a striptease in a wheelchair; the group's tagline is "An unashamed claim to beauty in the face of invisibility." "Each of these artists is in a non-normative body," said cofounder Patty Berne in 2009, "and each is a miraculous, sexual being." Put another way, as a commenter on Sins Invalid's website did: "HOT!" The comment opens the imagination to the broad, gorgeous, unexplored landscape of the erotic.

Another aspect of the tyranny of the normal: the demand that to be "healthy," everyone must be monogamously coupled, or just sexual. Writing on the Asexual Outreach site, Sam articulates what it's like to be asexual, or without sexual feelings, and the target of this edict: "We were told [sex] was a primal need, as essential as breathing, or drinking. Even certain psychologists and psychiatrists, in Freudian times, reduced the core being of any person to their sexual needs. These ideas were pummeled into our very minds. Ignorance was not bliss then; it made me a freak of nature, a monster, something wrong and broken." Organizations like the Asexual Visibility and Education Network allow us to imagine other ways of being satisfied and whole, whether sexual or not.

In a project like this book, which sets its sights on naming, responding to, and ending gender violence, it is sometimes hard to proclaim that pleasure is no less worthy of our passionate advocacy than safety. That is what these organizers, bloggers, and lovers are doing with their body-liberating, feminist, and intersectional politics. Less obviously, these pleasure activists stress that it is not just in shared principles and vision that movements for justice cohere, and it's not only through (that wearying word) struggle that they progress. The political work we do together generates connection, intimacy, and happiness. It renews us with what Audre Lorde called, in the most inclusive way, the erotic:

> For the erotic is not a question only of what we do; it is a question of how acutely and fully we can feel in the doing. Once we know the extent to which we are capable of feeling that sense of satisfaction and completion, we can then observe which of our various life endeavors bring us closest to that fullness.

As a working-class, Caribbean-American lesbian, Lorde experienced her share of pain. But in her art, her activism, and her very presence, she loved her body and her desires, out loud: "Within the celebration of the erotic in all our endeavors, my work becomes a conscious decision, a longed-for bed which I enter gratefully and from which I rise up empowered."[7]

# 7

# Build and Sustain a Robust Welfare State, Not a Carceral State

### Invest in Education, Arts, and Health Care. Divest from Policing and Prisons.

The punishment industry is always hiring. Each year, the United States "spends over $100 billion on police and over $50 billion on the judiciary," political scientist Marie Gottschalk reminds us in *Caught: The Prison State and the Lockdown of American Politics*. "One in eight state employees works in corrections."[1] And that's just the government.

The United States also employs more guards per capita than any other industrialized nation: in 2011, 5.2 million people worked in what economists Samuel Bowles and Arjun Jayadev call "guard labor"—private security guards, police, soldiers and civil military workers, prison and court officials, or weapons manufacturers.[2] The claim is that the TSA agents and school metal detector operators are keeping everyone safe. But what's really happening is that some people are protecting themselves, and their stuff, from other people. More "protective services" are linked with more inequality.

Decades of austerity and regressive tax policies have created this inequality by transferring wealth to the very top from everyone else, and from public to private hands. In the United States, private capital is five times the amount of public capital, and net public wealth is below zero, according to the World Inequality Database.[3] The emptying of public coffers leaves the government unable to care for its citizens. And when now-scarce resources flow to hospital surveillance cameras instead of to nurses, people are actually less safe.

Along with income, the distribution of danger and risk is radically unequal. A school in a low-income community of color has detention but no after-school program. If the parents cannot afford a babysitter, those students are on their own when the school day ends. And nonwhite parents have another worry: their children will be perceived as threats, not as threatened, arrested for "loitering," or reported to police by white neighbors for having a pool party or mowing a lawn—with the intention of keeping the streets safe, of course.

All this is part of what German sociologist Ulrich Beck calls the risk society. The risk society is one in which people, through technology and capitalism—and we would add, white supremacist policies—create catastrophic hazards like global warming and economic precarity, and then turn to technology, capitalism, and authoritarian government to manage the risk and "protect" us from the harms of those human-made catastrophes.

The sex offense legal regime is a perfect example of the risk society because the risks it manages are those it has produced itself. Each costly technology purported to manage risk—public registry, amber alerts—adds to the sense of an ever-present, uncontrolled, and uncontrollable menace: the "predator." Rather than encouraging us to look after each other's children, it recruits neighbors to inform on any adult who might enjoy hanging with children. The fear business, as Beck calls it—merchants of nannycams or Tasers—rakes it in.[4]

If all this sounds insane, that's because it is. But the solution is not so complicated. If regressive tax policies send the wealth upward and impoverish the treasury, progressive taxes can redistribute wealth widely and replenish the resources needed, so people are not just safe but thriving. A socialist economy does this even better. Rather than trying to rectify a vastly unequal outcome, it aims to create equality from the get-go.

A robust welfare state is a feminist vision: a vision of mutual aid and care, not mutual suspicion and punishment; one of libraries and doulas, free national parks, college, and childcare, and environmentally clean public transport. A robust welfare state is one in which you walk into a clinic with a broken arm and they put your arm in a cast, period. When a hurricane floods your city, an army of sanitation workers and carpenters arrives the next day.

These demands are not new. The 1963 March on Washington

for Jobs and Freedom demanded full employment and a minimum wage that was a living wage. Socialist feminists of the 1970s pushed for well-funded social services and benefits. These demands are not excessive. Every wealthy nation—and some not-so-wealthy ones—has the essentials of a welfare state (though these, too, are imperiled by austerity and growing inequality). Yes, we face a uniquely American challenge: the word "welfare" is not neutral. But a recent Gallup poll sends good news: most young adults prefer socialism to capitalism.[5] So do we, emphatically.

We endorse a welfare state, even though the boundaries between social services and policing are often fluid—something intimately familiar to low-income women who must negotiate hostile institutions to keep their children or access benefits. Our vision is not of systems that use care and protection to punish; it is not of a state that gives (or revokes) "charity" to those its economy has abandoned, or in the case of the African American descendants of slaves, those it has deliberately enclosed and targeted as disposable.

Where a nation puts its money is the concrete expression of its priorities. Its economic system enacts its values: capitalism worships profit, which means the exploitation of the many for the benefit of the few. Neoliberalism, the religious belief that the marketplace solves every problem, abandons all responsibility to those left behind in brutal twenty-first-century capitalism. US capitalism was born in genocide, dispossession, and slavery. White supremacism, including the criminalization and economic exclusion of nonwhite people, is intrinsic to the enduring power of the US economy; the two cannot be disentangled. If we want to end violence and protect children, we have to divest from the industries of punishment and surveillance and invest in what allows people and communities to flourish. And to invest in those things we need economic, political, and social systems that put people—all people—before profit.

# 8

# Think Intersectionally

## Organize across Differences

> *"There is no such thing as a single-issue struggle because we do not live single-issue lives. Malcolm knew this. Martin Luther King Jr. knew this. Our struggles are particular, but we are not alone."*
>
> Audre Lorde
>
> Address at Harvard University, 1982[1]

It should by now go without saying—but we will say it again: any successful movement must be intersectional, because we are all intersectional beings. Race, class, gender, sexuality, or ability cannot be separated from one another in thinking about people, systems, or politics. Nativists, racists, and the state's punitive bureaucracy can defeat intersectionality by assigning labels—"illegal alien," "felon," "pedophile"—that flatten identities to one vilified thing. If kept apart, groups of people are inevitably marginalized, and fissures open that resist healing. Movements falter.

No movement can understand what it's up against, or how to fight back, if it doesn't locate itself at the crossroads of identities, situations, and oppressions. But intersectionality is not simply about mashing as many "categories" of person into your movement as possible. It is more than recognizing difference and kinship and keeping both central in analyses and actions. We need to make sure that it does not fall to those who experience the most harm to make the intersectional connections—"to be the damn bridge to everybody," as Donna Kate Rushin put it in 1981, in the opening poem of her germinal collection *This Bridge Called My Back*.[2] White people must do the work to unlearn and dismantle white supremacy, just as cisgender, heterosexual men must challenge patriarchy without waiting for women and queers to do it. "Stretch or drown. Evolve or die," wrote Rushin. That means everybody.

Finally—although this may seem contradictory—we should not forget that working across difference sometimes means creating spaces for "your people" only, however those boundaries are drawn. Affinity groups, identity caucuses, or QTPOC (queer and trans, plus people of color) events that give succor, skills, and strength to some are necessary to building movements that can liberate us all.

# 9

# Practice Restorative and Transformative Justice

## Create Community Responses to Harm outside the Carceral State

Yes, registries must be dismantled, and we must stop the proliferation of laws and policies that brand and isolate increasing numbers of "sex offenders" yet do nothing to make our communities safer. But these moves alone will not diminish sexual violence. Eliminating bad laws is necessary but not sufficient.

Whether we call our work restorative justice, transformative justice, or community accountability—and there are differences among them—we need paradigm shifts: from justice as retribution to justice as healing, from conviction to accountability, punishment to repair, and rehabilitation to transformation. Movements for transformative and restorative justice are not just for institutions, nonprofits, or, simply, someone else. All of us need to step away from the systems to which we have outsourced the responsibility to deal with harm and make us safer.

Reading a lot, and having all the right theories, isn't enough either. "Many spend so much time online and in movement spaces perfecting the language about the politic," says Shira Hassan of the Just Practice transformative justice network. "I don't care what your politic is if you aren't practicing. The practice makes the politic real."

Schoolteachers and administrators, working with creative collectives of educators, can rethink school protocols, retrain faculty, engage students and parents in restorative practices as well as social and emotional learning, and speak and listen in ways that deal with conflict and harm while building peaceful, cooperative school communities. Social workers can follow Article 5 of the

1968 Position Statement from the National Association of Black Social Workers: "We direct white social workers to involve themselves in solving the problem of white racism—America's number one mental health problem."[1] We can get started wherever we are. We can't wait for our bosses to give us permission.

A multitude of small transformative justice initiatives worldwide are propagating new ways to organize to stop sexual violence before it happens and to respond more constructively when it does, without policing or punishment. As people learn the practical and personal skills of mutual aid and conflict resolution, as they gain confidence in each other, they can let go of dependency on the current criminal legal system and the fear that they will be in danger without it.

Are these practices always perfect, effective, or "right"? No. But they are taking us in the right direction.

# 10

# Embrace Abolition Feminism

In 2016, Sarah Reed, a thirty-two-year-old multiracial woman, was found dead in her cell at Holloway Prison, on the outskirts London, then the largest women's prison in Western Europe. Four years earlier, Reed had been accused of shoplifting and assaulted by a white police officer. Inside prison, like other prisoners of color, she was thrown into segregation and denied medical care and essential psychiatric medications. Abolition feminists, along with Black Lives Matter and #SayHerName, memorialized Reed's life and raged against her death, which one organizer, Lee Jasper, called "a horrific tale of institutional racism, sexual violence, corruption and brutal incompetence/negligence that defies belief."[1]

The next year, the government decided to close the prison, disperse the incarcerated women further from the city and their families, and sell this public land—now prime real estate in a gentrifying neighborhood—to luxury developers to fund building more prisons. Reclaim Holloway—a coalition of feminists, anti-prison and anti-racism activists, and community organizers, led by the grassroots network Sisters Uncut—demanded that the land be turned into gardens and playgrounds and the building into affordable housing and a women's center. Reclaim Holloway is a transformational movement. On these several acres, it aims to remake a place of hardship and isolation into one of well-being and community. Instead of allowing the erasure of the thousands of women and girls who have been confined there, including the women's suffragists of the early twentieth century, the proposed women's center honors them.[2]

This is abolition feminism, a melding of anti-racist prison abolitionism—which is part of the Black radical tradition—and feminism. It grows out of the recognition of the shared ideologies that undergird state violence and interpersonal gender violence and the official and cultural conflation of vengeance with justice. This analysis goes back nearly a half century in the United States. An early white exponent was the white Quaker pacifist Fay Honey Knopp, whose Prison Research Education Action Project published the remarkably prescient *Instead of Prisons: A Handbook for Abolitionists* in 1976. Later, PREAP was repurposed as the Safer Society Project, a leading publisher and clearinghouse of resources on sexual abuse and violence. "The issue of sexual abuse and how society responds to it is an abolitionist issue," Knopp wrote in *Peace Journal* in 1994. "After *Instead of Prisons*, I wanted to look at one of the more serious behaviors, sexual offenses, and examine their effect, their roots in the social structure, and their relationship to more global issues." Knopp added: "I wanted to look at primary prevention [and] find something we could do, hands on, to reduce the harm done both to victims/survivors and to offenders."[3]

At the beginning of this century, this dual strategy—investigating the roots and global implications of violence and doing the hands-on work of preventing and repairing it—began to coalesce into the politics and practices of transformative justice. The 2001 INCITE!/Critical Resistance Statement called on organizers to "make connections between interpersonal violence, the violence inflicted by domestic state institutions (such as prisons, detention centers, mental hospitals, and child protective services), and international violence (such as war, military base sex work, and nuclear testing)." The statement garnered the signatures of scores of organizations and hundreds of individuals.[4]

A dozen years later, at the University of Chicago, Angela Davis joined abolition and feminism again, calling them "essential theories for the twenty-first century." Davis's political consciousness—her feminism, communism, and commitment to the liberation of all people—had been forged, like that of so many Black radicals of her generation, under the combined forces of personal and state violence. During a childhood in Birmingham, Alabama, she had witnessed racial segregation murderously enforced by both government authorities and vigilantes; as an organizer in the Black Power movement she counted the Black casualties of the FBI's war of incarceration and assassination against the movement's leaders, and was incarcerated herself.

In the 2013 talk, Davis lifted up transwomen, who have "worked out a deeply feminist approach . . . at the intersection of race, class, sexuality, and gender." Fighting to be included in the category "woman," they are transforming that category, she said, as women of color transformed the feminisms of the early 1970s. At the same time, transwomen are "harassed, arrested, and incarcerated, primarily in male prisons, where they are marked as targets of male violence." Their struggles and resistance show us that people who fight against prisons "must also embrace the abolition of gender policing"; that "the people on the front lines against violence against women should also be on the front line of abolitionist struggles," and that those "opposed to police crimes should be opposed to domestic—privatized—violence."[5] In this talk Davis used the term abolition (some say abolitionist) feminism, a concept that has ricocheted through political discourses, practices, and coalitions around the world.

If we are to end sexual violence and dismantle the carceral state and the sex offense legal regime, we need a fundamental recalibration of politics as usual. Even if they are not going to work directly with each other, movements that have not seen themselves as allies can learn solidarity: anti-violence feminists with prison abolitionists; those supporting the sexually harmed with those fighting for the rights of people who have done sexual harm. For freedom and transformation, for accountability and repair, and for the proliferation of pleasures, we look toward the next messy, exhilarating chapter in the creation of a world where all can flourish. Abolition feminism can get us there.

# Acknowledgments

**Erica**: While all of my work benefits from being in community and struggle with others, during the years this project germinated I had the opportunity to learn from many brilliant folks whose thinking, practice, writing, and feedback strengthened this book, including Amanda Agan, Tammy Bond, David Booth, Monica Cosby, Angela Davis, Gina Dent, Treva Ellison, Erica Friscioni, Laurie Fuller, Gillian Harkins, Shira Hassan, Jess Heaney, Guy Hamilton-Smith, Jean Hughes, Rachel Herzing, Mariame Kaba, Alice Kim, Mimi Kim, Debbie Kilroy, Jason Lydon, Meenakshi Mannoe, Toshio Meronek, Nuri Nusrat, Therese Quinn, Fran Royster, Ann Russo, Eric Stanley, Cassandra Shaylor, Charandev Singh, Dean Spade, Amita Swadhin, Megan Selby, Laurie Schaffner, Melissa Tanis, Emily Thuma, Beth Richie, and Wes Ware.

My contributions to this project also reflect learning from many organizations, including the Bay Area Transformative Justice Network; Bent Bars; Black and Pink; Black Youth Project 100; Building Communities, Ending Violence; Critical Resistance; Generation Five; INCITE! Women, Gender Non-Conforming, and Trans People of Color Against Violence; Just Practice; Mirror Memoirs; Project Nia; Storytelling and Organizing Project / Creative Interventions; Transformative Justice Kollektiv Berlin; Young Women's Empowerment Project; and multiple small and large gatherings on abolition, transformative justice and ending gender and sexual violence.

Most importantly, this project was only possible because of Judith Levine's humor, expertise, and labor.

**Judith**: First, big love and thanks to Erica, whose organizing experience and political wisdom inspire and educate me and give heft and heart to this book. To the staff, volunteers, and circle participants at the Hardwick, Vermont, Community Justice Center; the Ahimsa Collective and other learners and teachers in the Restorative Approaches to Sexual Harm and the Patriarchy training; Mika Dashman, who first told me about RJ; and my co–board members and fellow travelers of the National Center for Reason and Justice: Debbie Nathan, Mike Snedeker, Roger Lancaster, Frank Kane, Bob Chatelle, Jim d'Entremont, and especially Emily Horowitz and Bill Dobbs. Some of the people who helped me think and/or pay the rent were (in alphabetical order) Deb Chasman, Mandeep Dhaliwal, Laurie Essig, Willa Farrell, Kim Fellner, Kathy Fox, Vivian Gornick, Trevor Hoppe, Debbie Nathan, Nuri Nusrat, Joan Rappaport, Nausicaa Renner, Dana Tortorici, and Suzi Wizowaty. Paul Cillo reminds me there's still fun to be had in this sorry world. Ann Snitow was a beloved friend, comrade, encourager, and unparalleled feminist intellectual and organizer. I dedicate this book to her and will miss her every day.

We both thank Rosie Warren, Andy Hsiao, Duncan Ranslem, and Ben Mabie at Verso, as well as copyeditor Sam Smith; Joy Harris and Adam Reed at the Joy Harris Literary Agency; and the Open Society Foundations' Soros Justice Fellowship program, which supported the project out of which this book evolved.

# Notes

## Introduction

1 Sonia Moghe and Lauren de Valle, "Larry Nassar's abuse victims, in their own words," CNN, January 17, 2018, cnn.com/2018/01/16/us/nassar-victim-impact-statements.
2 Scott Cacciola and Victor Mather, "Larry Nassar sentencing: 'I just signed your death warrant,'" *New York Times*, January 24, 2018, nytimes.com/2018/01/24/sports/larry-nassar-sentencing.
3 Even the least punitive states in the United States rank alongside countries such as Turkmenistan, Thailand, Rwanda, and Russia, which "have authoritarian governments or have recently experienced large-scale internal armed conflicts." Peter Wagner and Wendy Sawyer, "States of Incarceration: The Global Context 2018," Prison Policy Initiative, June 2018, prisonpolicy.org; Aleks Kajstura, "The States of Women's Incarceration: The Global Context 2018," Prison Policy Initiative, November 2018, prisonpolicy.org.
4 The BJS survey of 90,000 households included both reported and unreported crimes. US Bureau of Justice Statistics, *National Crime Victims Survey 2017* (Washington, DC: US Bureau of Justice Statistics, 2017), bjs.gov/index.cfm?ty=dcdetail&iid=245.
5 Kelly Hayes and Miriame Kabe, "The Sentencing of Larry Nassar Was Not 'Transformative Justice,'" *Appeal*, February 5, 2018, theappeal.org/the-sentencing-of-larry-nassar-was-not-transformative-justice-here-s-why.
6 Amanda Y. Agan, "Sex Offender Registries: Fear without Function?," *Journal of Law and Economics* 54:1 (2011), 207–39; Jill S. Levenson, "Restricting Sex Offender Residences: Policy Implications," *Human Rights Magazine*, June 30, 2017, americanbar.org/groups/crsj/publications/human_rights_magazine_home/human_rights_vol36_2009/spring2009/restriciting_sex_offender_residences_policy_implications.
7 Centers for Disease Control, *National Intimate Partner and Sexual Violence Survey (NISVS): An Overview of 2010 Summary Report Findings* (Washington, DC: Centers for Disease Control, 2010), 18, cdc.gov/violenceprevention/pdf/nisvs_report2010-a.pdf.
8 Rachel E. Morgan and Grace Kena, *Criminal Victimization: 2016, Revised* (October 2018) (Washington, DC: US Bureau of Justice Statistics, 2018), NCJ 252121.

9 See, e.g., Rosaleen McElvaney, Shiela Greene, and Diane Hogan, "To Tell or Not to Tell: Factors Influencing Young People's Informal Disclosures of Child Sexual Abuse," *Journal of Interpersonal Violence* 29:5 (2014), 928–47. Disclosure rates may be understated because disclosure is not a discrete event, but more often partial, iterative, or delayed. Ramona Alaggia, Delphine Collin-Vézina, and Rusan Lateef, "Facilitators and Barriers to Child Sexual Abuse (CSA) Disclosures: A Research Update (2000–2016)," *Trauma, Violence, and Abuse* 20:2 (2019) 260–83.

10 CDC, *National Intimate Partner and Sexual Violence Survey*, 20.

11 Tessa Berenson, "1 in 5: Debating the Most Controversial Sexual Assault Statistic," *Time*, June 27, 2014, time.com/2934500/1-in-5%e2%80%82campus-sexual-assault-statistic.

12 Sofi Sinozich and Lynn Langton, *Rape and Sexual Assault Victimization among College-Age Females, 1995–2013* (Washington, DC: US Bureau of Justice Statistics, 2014), NCJ 248471.

13 Wendy Ruderman, "Crime Report Manipulation Is Common Among New York Police, Study Finds," *New York Times*, June 29, 2012, nytimes.com/2012/06/29/nyregion/new-york-police-department-manipulates-crime-reports-study-finds.html.

14 Philip M. Stinson et al., "Police Sexual Misconduct: A National Scale Study of Arrested Officers," *Criminal Justice Faculty Publications*, Paper 30 (2014), bwjp.org/assets/documents/pdfs/webinars/dhhs-police-sexual-misconduct-a-national-scale-study.pdf.

15 These women and many others have been supported and their fates publicized by Survived and Punished, a national coalition of survivors, advocates, attorneys, policy experts, and currently and formerly incarcerated people, which organizes to "de-criminalize survival . . . support and free criminalized survivors, and abolish gender violence, policing, prisons, and deportations." Survived and Punished, survivedandpunished.org.

16 Holly Yan and Madeline Holcombe, "A Pregnant Woman Shot in the Stomach Is Indicted in Her Unborn Child's Death," *CNN*, June 28, 2019, cnn.com/2019/06/27/us/alabama-pregnant-woman-shot-in-stomach-manslaughter-indictment-trnd. After national protest, the state dropped the charges.

17 Debbie Nathan and Michael Snedeker, *Satan's Silence: Ritual Abuse and the Making of a Modern American Witch Hunt* (New York: Basic Books, 1995); Richard Beck, *We Believe the Children* (New York: PublicAffairs, 2015).

18 Peter Wagner and Wendy Sawyer, *Mass Incarceration: The Whole Pie 2019*, Slide 5, Prison Policy Initiative, March 19, 2019, prisonpolicy.org/reports/pie2019.html#slideshows/slideshow5/3.

19 These include Florida, Louisiana, Montana, Texas, and others that have had their laws overturned. Alabama's legislature passed such a law in June 2019. Elizabeth Thomas, "Alabama Lawmakers Pass Bill Requiring Chemical Castration for Child Sex Offenders," *ABC*, June 5, 2019.

20 There is evidence that this is an overcount, including double entries of people living in other states, incarcerated, deported, or dead. Alissa R. Ackerman, Jill S. Levenson, and Andrew Harris, "How Many Sex Offenders Really Live among Us? Adjusted Counts and Population Rates in Five US States," *Journal of Crime and Justice* 35:3 (2012), 464–74, doi.org/10.1080/0735648X.2012.666407.

21 Restoration of Rights Project, "Relief from Sex Offender Registry Obligations," Collateral Consequences Research Center, November 1, 2017, ccresourcecenter.org/state-restoration-profiles/50-state-comparison-relief-from-sex-offender-registration-obligations.

22 In the case of an Oklahoma man on the federal registry returned to prison for a violation of parole, the Supreme Court ruled in June 2019 that only a jury, not a judge, has the power to determine criminal conduct and apply additional penalty. *United States v. Hammond* 588 US_2019, supreme.justia.com/cases/federal/us/588/17-1672/#tab-opinion-4113752.

23 Miriam Zoila Pérez, "What Would It Take to Actually End Intimate Violence?" *Colorlines*, November 28, 2017, colorlines.com/articles/what-would-it-take-actually-end-intimate-violence.

24 Angela Y. Davis, "Feminism and Abolition: Theories and Practices for the Twenty-First Century," address given at the University of Chicago, May 2013, youtube.com/watch?v=koieCAUWGnM.

## 1 Anti-violence Feminisms

1 Noreen Connell and Cassandra Wilson, *Rape: The First Sourcebook for Women* (New York: New York Radical Feminists, 1974), 242.

2 Ibid., 125.

3 Elizabeth Bernstein, *Temporarily Yours: Intimacy, Authenticity, and the Commerce of Sex* (Chicago: University of Chicago Press, 2007), 143.

4 European Women's Lobby, "The Price of Austerity: The Impact on Women's Rights and Gender Equality" (Brussels: Creative Commons, 2012), 8, 10.

5 N. Zoe Hilton, Grant T. Harris, and Marnie E. Rice, "The Effect of Arrest on Wife Assault Recidivism: Controlling for Pre-arrest Risk," *Criminal Justice and Behavior* 34:10 (2007), 1334.

6 Reentry and Housing Coalition, "Homelessness—What We Know," reentryandhousing.org/public-housing. See also Cora Currier, "Organizing Skid Row," *Dissent* (Summer 2019), 89–95.

7 Kate Pickert, "What's Wrong with the Violence against Women Act?," *Time*, February 27, 2013, nation.time.com/2013/02/27/whats-wrong-with-the-violence-against-women-act.

8 HR 6545, 115th Congress, 2nd session (2018), as introduced, congress.gov/bill/115th-congress/house-bill/6545/text.

9 Donna Coker, "Shifting Power for Battered Women: Law, Material Resources, and Poor Women of Color," *UC Davis Law Review* 33:1009 (2000), 1046–47. See also Beth Richie, *Arrested Justice: Black Women, Violence, and America's Prison Nation* (New York: NYU Press, 2012) for an insightful critique of anti-violence movements' engagement with the state.

10 Emily Yoffe, "The Question of Race in Campus Sexual-Assault Cases," *Atlantic*, September 11, 2017, theatlantic.com/education/archive/2017/09/the-question-of-race-in-campus-sexual-assault-cases/539361. Yoffe also provides convincing anecdotal evidence of racial disparities in the adjudication of these cases.

11 Tessa Berenson, "The Country Is Torn over Betsy DeVos' New Campus Sexual Assault Guidelines," *Time*, September 22, 2017, time.com/4954158/betsy-devos-title-ix-sexual-assault-guidelines. See also Lara Bazelon, "I'm a Democrat and a Feminist. And I Support Betsy DeVos's Title IX Reforms," *New York Times*, December 4, 2018, nytimes.com/2018/12/04/opinion/-title-ix-devos-democrat-feminist.html.

12 Irina D. Manta, "Commentary: Do You Lie on Tinder? There Should Be a Law about That," *Chicago Tribune*, November 20, 2018, chicagotribune.com/news/opinion/commentary/ct-perspec-tinder-lies-online-dating-fraud-laws-1123-20181120-story.html.

13 Alexandra Brodsky, "Rape-Adjacent: Imagining Legal Responses to Nonconsensual Condom Removal," *Columbia Journal of Gender and Law* 32:2 (2017), 183–210.

14 Sherry F. Colb, "The Jewish 'Rape by Deception' Case: Can a Lie Transform Consensual Sex into Rape?," *FindLaw*, August 4, 2010, supreme.findlaw.com/legal-commentary/the-jerusalem-rape-by-deception-case-can-a-lie-transform-consensual-sex-into-rape.html; Sophie Wilkinson, "The Troubling Case of a UK Woman Convicted of 'Gender Fraud,'" *Vice*, December 22, 2017, vice.com/en_ca/article/43qvz9/the-troubling-case-of-a-uk-woman-convicted-of-gender-fraud.

15 Susan Chira and Catrin Einhorn, "How Tough Is It to Change a Culture of Harassment? Ask the Women at Ford," *New York Times*, December 19, 2017, nytimes.com/interactive/2017/12/19/us/ford-chicago-sexual-harassment.html.

## 2 Intersectionality

1 Angela Y. Davis, quoted in Maria Bevacqua, *Rape on the Public Agenda: Feminism and the Politics of Sexual Assault* (Boston: Northeastern University Press, 2000), 39.

2 Ibid., 78.

3 Jane Loader, "Exposing the Rapist Next Door," *Seven Days*, April 25, 1977.

4 Combahee River Collective, "Combahee River Collective Statement," April 1977, available at: americanstudies.yale.edu/sites/default/files/files/Keyword%20Coalition_Readings.pdf.
5 Kimberlé Williams Crenshaw, "Demarginalizing the Intersection of Race and Sex: A Black Feminist Critique of Anti-discrimination Doctrine, Feminist Theory, and Anti-racist Politics," *University of Chicago Legal Forum* 1:8 (1989), 139–67.
6 INCITE! and Critical Resistance, "Statement on Gender Violence and the Prison-Industrial Complex," 2001, incite-national.org/incite-critical-resistance-statement.

## 3 Protecting (White) "Innocence"

1 Bill Lichtenstein, interview by Judith Levine, February 2015.
2 Kathryn Bond Stockton, *The Queer Child, or Growing Sideways in the Twentieth Century* (Durham: Duke University Press, 2009), 16. For a discussion of the history of the racial formation of childhood and innocence, see Robin Bernstein, *Racial Innocence: Performing American Childhood from Slavery to Civil Rights* (New York: NYU Press, 2011).
3 Rebecca Epstein, Jamilia J. Blake, and Thalia González, "Girlhood Interrupted: The Erasure of Black Girls' Childhood," Georgetown Law Center for Poverty and Inequality, n.d., 4, law.georgetown.edu/poverty-inequality-center/wp-content/uploads/sites/14/2017/08/girlhood-interrupted.pdf. Native American girls are detained nine times as often as their white counterparts for status offenses. Coalition for Juvenile Justice, "Girls, Status Offenses, and the Need for a Less Punitive and More Empowering Approach," Coalition for Juvenile Justice, n.d., 4, juvjustice.org/our-work/safety-opportunity-and-success-project/issue-areas/girls.

## 4 Punishment and "Management": The Sex Offender Registry

1 Linh Ta, "The Missing Kids Milk Carton Campaign Started in Iowa," *Des Moines Register*, September 4, 2017, desmoinesregister.com/story/news/crime-and-courts/2017/09/04/missing-kids-milk-carton-campaign-outcome/627165001; "Milk Carton Kids," *99 Percent Invisible*, Radiotopia, September 15, 2015, 99percentinvisible.org/episode/milk-carton-kids.
2 "Kidnapped Children Make Headlines, but Abductions Are Rare in US," *Reuters*, January 11, 2019, reuters.com/article/us-wisconsin

-missinggirl-data/kidnapped-children-make-headlines-but-abduction-is-rare-in-u-s-idUSKCN1P52BJ.

3 Warwick Cairns, *How to Live Dangerously* (New York: St. Martins, 2009), 45.

4 Marie Gottschalk, *Caught: The Prison State and the Lockdown of American Politics* (Princeton: Princeton University Press, 2016), 199.

5 Adam Walsh Child Protection and Safety Act, HR 4472 (2006), available at ncsl.org/research/civil-and-criminal-justice/adam-walsh-child-protection-and-safety-act.aspx.

6 Elizabeth J. Letourneau et al., "Evaluating the Effectiveness of Sex Offender Registration and Notification Policies for Reducing Sexual Violence Against Women," Medical University of South Carolina, 2010, ncjrs.gov/pdffiles1/nij/grants/231989.pdf.

7 Eli Lehrer, "Rethinking Sex Offender Registries," *National Review* (Winter 2016).

8 Michael Hobbes, "Sex Offender Registries Don't Keep Kids Safe, but Politicians Keep Expanding Them Anyway," *HuffPost*, July 16, 2019, huffpost.com/entry/sex-offender-laws-dont-make-children-safer-politicians-keep-passing-them-anyway_n_5d2c8571e4b02a5a5d5e96d1.

9 *Millard v. Rankin,* 265 F.Supp.3d 1211 (2017).

10 Colorado Supreme Court, *Colorado in the Interest of T.B.* (June 17, 2019). See Michael Roberts, "Colorado Sex Offender Registry Takes Another Brutal Hit," *Westword*, June 21, 2019, westword.com/news/colorado-juvenile-sex-offenders-lifetime-registration-loses-key-case-11387044.

11 US District Court Middle District Alabama, Northern Div., *John Doe et al. v. Steven T. Marshall et al.*, Order (February 11, 2019). See Jacob Sullum, "'Sex Offenders Are Not Second-Class Citizens,' says US Judge While Nixing Alabama Rules on First Amendment Grounds," *Reason*, February 13, 2019, reason.com/2019/02/13/sex-offenders-are-not-second-class-citiz.

12 Patrick A. Langan, Erica L. Schmitt, and Matthew R. Durose, *Recidivism of Sex Offenders Released from Prison in 1994* (Washington, DC: US Bureau of Justice Statistics, November 16, 2003), NCJ 198281, bjs.gov/index.cfm?ty=pbdetail&iid=1136. For a bibliography of research on sex offender recidivism, see Women Against Registry, "Recidivism," n.d., womenagainstregistry.org/recidivism.

13 Ira Mark Ellman and Tara Ellman, "'Frightening and High': The Supreme Court's Crucial Mistake about Sex Crimes Statistics," *Constitutional Commentary* 30:3 (2015).

14 *Packingham v. North Carolina*, 137 S. Ct. 1730 (2017), casetext.com/case/packingham-v-north-carolina-1.

15 Franca Cortoni, Kelly M. Babchishin, and Clemence Rat, "The Proportion of Sexual Offenders Who Are Female Is Higher Than Thought: A Meta-Analysis," *Criminal Justice and Behavior* 44:2 (2017), 145–162, doi.org/10.1177/0093854816658923.

16 Alissa R. Ackerman et al., "Who Are the People in Your Neighborhood? A Descriptive Analysis of Individuals on Public Sex Offender Registries,"

*International Journal of Law and Psychiatry* 34:3 (2011) 149–59, doi: 10.1016/j.ijlp.2011.04.001.

17 Ibid.

18 "Race and Wrongful Convictions in the United States," National Registry of Exonerations, University of California, Irvine, March 7, 2017, available at law.umich.edu/special/exoneration/Documents/Race_and_Wrongful_Convictions.pdf.

19 Static-99 Coding Form (2016), available at static99.org.

20 Grant Duwe, William Donnay, and Richard Tewksbury, "Does Residential Proximity Matter? A Geographic Analysis of Sex Offense Recidivism," *Criminal Justice and Behavior* 35:4 (2008), 484–504.

21 J. C. Sandler, N. J. Freeman, and K. M. Socia, "Does a Watched Pot Boil? A Time-Series Analysis of New York State's Sex Offender Registration and Notification Law," *Psychology, Public Policy, and Law* 14:4 (2008), 284–302, dx.doi.org/10.1037/a0013881.

22 Amanda Y. Agan, "Sex Offender Registries: Fear without Function?," *Journal of Law and Economics* 54:1 (2011), 207–39; Interview and email correspondence with ERM, January 2016.

## 5 Policing Deviance: What Is a "Sex Offender"?

1 Judith Levine, *Harmful to Minors: The Perils of Protecting Children from Sex* (Minneapolis: University of Minnesota Press, 2002), 48.

2 Liat Ben-Moshe, Chris Chapman, and Alison C. Carey, eds., *Disability Incarcerated: Imprisonment and Disability in the US and Canada* (New York: Palgrave MacMillan, 2014); Eric A. Stanley and Nat Smith, eds., *Captive Genders: Trans Embodiment and the Prison Industrial Complex* (Oakland: AK Press, 2011).

3 Holly Brewer, *By Birth or Consent: Children, Law, and the Anglo-American Revolution in Authority* (Chapel Hill: Omohundro Institute and University of North Carolina Press, 2007), 288.

4 Coalition for Juvenile Justice / SOS Project, "Standards of Care for Non-Delinquent Youth," n.d., juvjustice.org/our-work/safety-opportunity-and-success-project/national-standards/section-i-principles-responding-4.

5 "A Look at New Jersey's Controversial New Sex Law for Minors," *Children's Legal Rights Journal* 31 (1979–80); Kelsey Dumond, "Cast Me Not Away! The Plight of Modern Day Romeo and Juliet," *Quinnipiac Law Review* 36:3 (2018), 455–87.

6 Judith Levine, "A Question of Abuse," *Mother Jones*, July/August 1996.

7 See, e.g., Toni Cavanagh Johnson and Carmen Berry, "Children Who Molest: A Treatment Program," *Journal of Interpersonal Violence* 4:2 (June 1989), 185–203.

8 David Finkelhor, Richard Ormrod, and Mark Chaffin, "Juveniles Who Commit Sex Offenses against Minors," *Juvenile Justice Bulletin* (December 2009), 2, unh.edu/ccrc/pdf/CV171.pdf.

9 Michael F. Caldwell, "Quantifying the Decline in Juvenile Sexual Recidivism Rates," *Psychology, Public Policy and Law* 22:4 (2016), 414–26.

10 Guttmacher Institute, "Sex and HIV Education," March 2019, guttmacher.org/state-policy/explore/sex-and-hiv-education.

11 Joey Mogul, Andrea Ritchie, and Kay Whitlock, *Queer (In)justice: The Criminalization of LGBT People in the United States* (Boston: Beacon, 2011); Angela Irvine, "'We've Had Three of Them': Addressing the Invisibility of Lesbian, Gay, Bisexual and Gender Nonconforming Youths in the Juvenile Justice System," *Columbia Journal of Gender and Law,* 19:3 (2010), 675–701; Irvine and Aisha M. Canfield, "The Overrepresentation of Lesbian, Gay, Bisexual, Questioning, Gender Nonconforming and Transgender Youth within the Child Welfare to Juvenile Justice Crossover Population," *Journal of Gender, Social Policy, and the Law*, 24:2 (2016), 243–61; Ilan H. Meyer et al., "Incarceration Rates and Traits of Sexual Minorities in the United States: National Inmate Survey, 2011–2012,"*American Journal Of Public Health* 107:2 (February 2017), 267–273, doi: 10.2105/AJPH.2016.303576.

12 Jaime M. Grant, Lisa A. Mottet, and Justin D. Tanis, "Injustice at Every Turn: A Report of the National Transgender Discrimination Survey," National LGBTQ Task Force, 2011, 5, available at static1.squarespace.com/static/566c7f0c2399a3bdabb57553/t/566cbf2c57eb8de92a5392e6/1449967404768/ntds_full.pdf.

13 Lambda Legal, "Protected and Served?," 2013, lambdalegal.org/protected-and-served.

14 "Incarceration Rates of LGBT People Three Times the General Population," UCLA School of Law Williams Institute, n.d., williamsinstitute.law.ucla.edu/williams-in-the-news/incarceration-rate-of-lesbian-gay-bisexual-people-three-times-the-general-population.

15 Haeyoun Park and Iaryna Mykhyalyshyn, "LGBT Individuals More Likely to Be Incarcerated," *New York Times*, June 16, 2016.

16 Gary J. Gates, "In US, More Adults Identifying as LGBT," *Gallup*, January 11, 2017, news.gallup.com/poll/201731/lgbt-identification-rises.aspx.

17 Jason Lydon et al., *Coming Out of Concrete Closest: A Report on Black and Pink's National LGBTQ Prisoner Survey*, October 2015, 4, docs.wixstatic.com/ugd/857027_fcd066f0c450418b95a18ab34647bd15.pdf.

18 Ellen Krug, "Skirting the Issues: Moose Lake," *Lavender Magazine*, July 6, 2017, lavendermagazine.com/our-affairs/skirting-the-issues-moose-lake.

19 Static-99 Coding Form (2016), available at static99.org.

20 Jason Parsley, "Kaitlyn Hunt Is Finally Free," *South Florida Gay News*, December 5, 2014, southfloridagaynews.com/Local/kaitlyn-hunt-is-engaged-and-pregnant.html.

21 Mercifully, this bill was defeated. House Bill 1688, Commonwealth of Massachusetts General Court, 186th Session (2008–2009), malegislature.gov/Bills/186/House/H1688.

22 "Neurodiversity" names the recognition and respect of neurological differences as human variations like any other. The neurodiverse may include those labeled with dyspraxia, dyslexia; attention deficit hyperactivity disorder, autism, and others.

23 Mark Mahoney, "Asperger's Syndrome and the Criminal Law: The Special Case of Child Pornography," 2009, available at harringtonmahoney.com.

24 Center for HIV Law and Policy, "HIV Criminalization in the US 2018," updated March 1, 2019, hivlawandpolicy.org/resources/map-hiv-criminalization-united-states-center-hiv-law-and-policy-2018.

25 See, e.g., Trevor Hoppe, *Punishing Disease: HIV and the Criminalization of Sickness* (Oakland: University of California Press, 2018).

26 Ruth Wilson Gilmore, "Race and Globalization," In R. J. Johnson, Peter J. Taylor, and Michael Watts, eds., *Geographies of Global Change: Remapping the World* (Hoboken: Wiley-Blackwell, 2002), 261–74.

27 Ibid., 180.

28 Joseph Shapiro, "NPR Investigation Finds Hidden Epidemic of Sexual Assault," *Morning Edition*, National Public Radio, January 8, 2018, npr.org/2018/01/08/576428410/npr-investigation-finds-hidden-epidemic-of-sexual-assault.

29 Joseph Shapiro, "States Aim to Halt Sexual Abuse of People with Intellectual Disabilities," *All Things Considered*, National Public Radio, June 28, 2018, npr.org/2018/06/25/623189167/states-aim-to-halt-sexual-abuse-of-people-with-intellectual-disabilities.

30 Sean Strub, "HIV: Prosecution or Prevention? HIV Is Not a Crime," in David M. Halperin and Trevor Hoppe, eds., *The War on Sex* (Durham: Duke University Press, 2017), 347–52.

31 Emily Bazelon, "The Price of a Stolen Childhood," *New York Times Magazine*, January 27, 2013, nytimes.com/2013/01/27/magazine/how-much-can-restitution-help-victims-of-child-pornography.html.

32 *New York v. Ferber*, 458 US 747 (1982).

33 Lawrence Stanley, "The Child Porn Myth," *Cardozo Arts and Entertainment Law Journal* 7 (1989), 313.

34 William Adams and Abigail Flynn, "Federal Prosecution of Commercial Sexual Exploitation of Children Cases, 2004–2013," (Washington, DC: Bureau of Justice Statistics, October 2017), NCJ 250746.

35 Amy Adler, "The Perverse Law of Child Pornography," *Columbia Law Review* 101:2 (2001), 209–72.

## 6 Medicalizing Violence

1 Kim English, "The Containment Approach: An Aggressive Strategy for the Community Management of Adult Sex Offenders" *Psychology, Public Policy, and Law* 4:1/2 (1998), 218–35.

2 Of 9,691 sex offenders released from prison in 1994, 5.3 percent were rearrested for a sex crime in the next three years and 3.5 percent were reconvicted. Patrick A. Langan, Erica L. Schmitt, and Matthew R. Durose, "Recidivism of Sex Offenders Released from Prison in 1994," (Washington, DC: US Bureau of Justice Statistics, 2003), NCJ 198281. In a Connecticut study tracking released sex offenders for five years, 2.7 percent were convicted of a new crime and 1.7 percent returned to prison. "Recidivism Among Sex Offenders in Connecticut," State of Connecticut Office of Policy and Management, 2012, ct.gov/opm/lib/opm/cjppd/cjresearch/recidivismstudy/sex_offender_recidivism_2012_final.pdf.

3 A few courts have ruled that the compelled admission of guilt and the confession of potentially illegal but unindicted acts violates the patient's Fifth Amendment protection against self-incrimination. Ashley Wheeler, Hal S. Wortzel, and Richard Martinez, "Required Sex Offender Treatment and Due Process Rights," *Journal of the American Academy of Psychiatry and the Law Online* 40:3 (September 2012), 435–7.

4 Texas Council on Sex Offender Treatment, "Difference Between Sex Offender Treatment and Psychotherapy," Texas Department of State Health Services, 2010, dshs.texas.gov/csot/csot_tdifference.shtm.

5 While in standard use in SOT, polygraphy, because of its variability and unreliability, is not admissible in court and is also rejected as unscientific by medical experts.

6 English, "The Containment Approach."

7 Peter Conrad and Joseph W. Schneider., *Deviance and Medicalization: From Badness to Sickness* (Oxford: Oxford University Press, 1980).

8 Stuart Kirk and Herb Kutchins, *Making Us Crazy: DSM, the Psychiatric Bible and the Creation of Mental Disorders* (New York: Free Press, 1997), 37–8; Daniel Goleman, "New Psychiatric Syndromes Spur Protest," *New York Times*, November 19, 1985, C1.

9 Janice K. Marques et al., "Effects of a Relapse Prevention Program on Sexual Recidivism: Final Results from California's Sex Offender Treatment and Evaluation Project (SOTEP)," *Sexual Abuse: A Journal of Research and Treatment* 17:1 (2005), 79–107.

10 American Psychiatric Association, *Dangerous Sexual Offenders: A Task Force Report of the American Psychiatric Association* (Washington, DC: American Psychiatric Association, 1999).

11 Stuart Scheingold, Toska Olson, and Jana Pershing, "The Politics of Sexual Psychopathy: Washington State's Sexual Predator Legislation," *Seattle University Law Review* 15:3 (1992), 809.

12 Wendy Sawyer and Peter Wagner, "Mass Incarceration: The Whole Pie 2019."

13 Amy Phenix et al., "Static 99R Coding Rules, Revised 2016," 36, static99.org/pdfdocs/Coding_manual_2016_InPRESS.pdf

14 Matt Henry, "Risk Assessment: Explained," *Appeal*, March 25, 2019, theappeal.org/risk-assessment-explained. See, e.g., Shoba Sreenivasan et al., "Alice in Actuarial-Land: Through the Looking Glass of Changing Static-99 Norms," *Journal of the American Academy of Psychiatry Law* 38:3 (2010), 400–6. A timeline of the "haphazard," "near constant state of flux" of the Static-99 can be found at forensicpsychologist.blogspot.com/2015/04/static-99-yet-more-bumps-on-rocky.html.

15 R. Karl Hanson and Kelly Morton-Bourgon, "Predictors of Sexual Recidivism: An Updated Meta-Analysis 2004–02," Public Works and Government Services Canada, Cat. No.: PS3-1/2004-2.

16 See, e.g., Richard Rogers and Rebecca L. Jackson, "Sexually Violent Predators: The Risky Enterprise of Risk Assessment," *Journal of the American Academy of Psychiatry and the Law* 33:4 (2005), 523–8; Julia Angwin et al., "Machine Bias," *ProPublica*, May 23, 2016, propublica.org/article/machine-bias-risk-assessments-in-criminal-sentencing; Erica R. Meiners, "How Risk Assessment Tools Are Condemning People to Indefinite Incarceration," *Truthout*, October 6, 2016, truthout.org/articles/how-risk-assessment-tools-are-condemning-people-to-indefinite-imprisonment.

17 Karl R. Hanson, "Long-Term Recidivism Studies Show That Desistance Is the Norm," *Criminal Justice and Behavior* 45:9 (2018), 1340–6.

18 Tamara Rice Lave and Justin McCrary, "Do Sexually Violent Predator Laws Violate Double Jeopardy or Substantive Due Process? An Empirical Inquiry," *Brooklyn Law Review* 78 (2013), 1392.

19 US District Court Eastern District of Missouri, *Van Orden v. Schafer*, Memorandum Order, September 11, 2015, available at themarshallproject.org/documents/2698309-Missouri-Ruling.

20 In the Interest of Jeremy Tim Johnson, Petitioner, 835 N.W.2d 806 (S. Ct. ND 2016).

21 *Karsjens v. Piper*, 845 F.3d 394 (2017), available at mitchellhamline.edu/sex-offense-litigation-policy/2017/07/20/karsjens-v-piper.

22 *Van Orden et al. v. Stringer et al.*, 262 F.Supp.3d 887 (E.D. Missouri 2017).

23 Kathryn J. Fox, "Civic Commitment: Promoting Desistance through Community Integration," *Punishment and Society* 18:1 (2016), 68–94.

24 Robin J. Wilson, Franca Cortoni, and Andrew J. McWhinnie, "Circles of Support and Accountability: A Canadian National Replication of Outcome Findings," *Sexual Abuse: A Journal of Research and Treatment* 21:4 (2009), 412–30.

25 Robin J. Wilson, Kathryn J. Fox, and Megan Kurmin, *CoSA in Vermont: Quantitative Outcomes and Qualitative Understandings*. Presentation at the 36th Annual Research and Treatment Conference of the

Association for the Treatment of Sexual Abusers, Kansas City, Missouri, 2017.

26 Grant Duwe, "Minnesota Circles of Support and Accountability (MnCoSA) at 50: Updated Results from a Randomized Controlled Trial," Minnesota Department of Corrections, February 2018, mn.gov/doc/assets/2018%20MnCOSA%20Outcome%20Evaluation_tcm1089-326700.pdf.

## 7 "Real" Guilt and the Trouble with Innocence

1 Sarah Stillman, "The List," *New Yorker*, March 14, 2016, newyorker.com/magazine/2016/03/14/when-kids-are-accused-of-sex-crimes.

2 Julie Bosman, "Teenager's Jailing Brings a Call to Fix Offender Registries," *New York Times*, July 4, 2015, A1.

3 "Ending the abusive practice of placing children on sex offender registries," Impact Justice, Center on Youth Registration Reform, impactjustice.org/impact/center-on-youth-registration-reform.

4 "States Slowly Scale Back Juvenile Sex Offender Registries," *Stateline*, November 19, 2015, pewtrusts.org/en/research-and-analysis/blogs/stateline/2015/11/19/states-slowly-scale-back-juvenile-sex-offender-registries.

5 George Steptoe and Antoine Goldet, "Why Some Young Sex Offenders Are Held Indefinitely," *Marshall Project*, January 27, 2016, themarshallproject.org/2016/01/27/why-some-young-sex-offenders-are-held-indefinitely.

## Racial or Gender or Class Justice?

1 Beth E. Richie, "How Anti-Violence Activism Taught Me to Become a Prison Abolitionist," *Feminist Wire*, January 2014, thefeministwire.com/2014/01/how-anti-violence-activism-taught-me-to-become-a-prison-abolitionist.

## 8 The "Sex Offenders'" Civil Rights Movement

1 *Packingham . North Carolina*, 582 US (2017); *Mutter v. Ross*, 16-1156 W. Va. (2018).

2 "Position Statement 55: Confining Sexual Predators in the Mental Health System," Mental Health America, mhanational.org/issues/position-statement-55-confining-sexual-predators-mental-health-system.

3 W. E. B. Du Bois, *Black Reconstruction in America: An Essay Toward a History of the Part Which Black Folk Played in the Attempt to Reconstruct Democracy in America, 1860–1880* (New York: Harcourt, Brace and Company, 1935).

4 Second Chances Florida, "Florida Voting Rights Restoration for Felons Initiative," available at secondchancesfl.org/about/voting-restoration-amendment. The initiative passed, but the Republican legislature has added the requirement that people pay all outstanding court fees and restitution, which can run into the tens of thousands of dollars, before being allowed to vote. Voting rights advocates are challenging this as a poll tax. Richard Luscombe, "The Voting Rights Advocates Fighting the Florida 'Poll Tax' on Former Felons," *Guardian,* July 25, 2019.

5 Barry Siegel, "Locking Up Sexual Predators," *Los Angeles Times*, May 10, 1990, Al.

6 American Civil Liberties, "ACLU Statement of Secretary DeVos's Proposed Rule on Title IX," November 16, 2018, aclu.org/press-release/aclu-statement-secretary-devoss-proposed-rule-title-ix.

7 Paul Wright, "Guest Column: Amendment 4 Doesn't Go Far Enough," *Florida Times-Union*, October 4, 2018, jacksonville.com/opinion/20181014/guest-column-amendment-4-doesnt-go-far-enough.

8 Deborah S. Esquenazi, *Southwest of Salem: The Story of the San Antonio Four*, (Austin: Deborah S. Esquenazi Productions, 2016).

9 "Bernard Baran," National Registry of Exonerations, University of California Irvine Newkirk Center for Science and Society, University of Michigan Law School, and Michigan State University College of Law, law.umich.edu/special/exoneration/Pages/casedetail.aspx?caseid=3011.

10 Ibid., "Margaret Kelly Michaels," law.umich.edu/special/exoneration/Pages/casedetail.aspx?caseid=3867.

11 Marie Malloy Parker, "Laverne Cox Distances Herself From Controversial Trans Inmate," *Advocate*, April 26, 2014, advocate.com/politics/transgender/2014/08/26/laverne-cox-distances-herself-controversial-trans-inmate.

12 Erica R. Meiners, "Never Innocent: Feminist Troubles with Sex Offender Registries and Protection in a Prison Nation," *Meridians: Feminism, Race, Transnationalism* 9 (2009), 34.

13 See, e.g., James Kilgore, "Repackaging Mass Incarceration," *Counterpunch*, June 6, 2014, counterpunch.org/2014/06/06/repackaging-mass-incarceration.

14 Paul Wright, "Amendment 4 Doesn't Go Far Enough."

15 Jason Lydon, "Message from Jason," *Black and Pink Newsletter*, April 2016, 2, issuu.com/blackandpink/docs/april_2016.

16 "Governor Brown Signs Bill Giving Right to Vote to Thousands Of Felons," KPIX-5, September 28, 2016, sanfrancisco.cbslocal.com/2016/09/28/gov-brown-signs-bill-giving-right-to-vote-to-felons-who-are-not-in-prison.

## 9 Religious Movements: Redemption, with Conditions

1 Tanya Erzen, *God in Captivity: The Rise of Faith-Based Prison Ministries in the Age of Mass Incarceration* (Boston: Beacon Press, 2017), 4–5.
2 Alexi Jones, "Cruel and Unusual: When States Don't Provide Air Conditioning in Prison," Prison Policy Initiative, June 18, 2019, prisonpolicy.org/blog/2019/06/18/air-conditioning.
3 Ruth Stout-Miller, Larry S. Miller, and Mary R. Langenbrunner, "Religiosity and Child Sexual Abuse: A Risk Factor Assessment," *Journal of Child Sexual Abuse* 6:4 (1998), 15–34.
4 Donna Eshuys and Stephen Smallbone, "Religious Affiliations among Adult Sexual Offenders," *Sexual Abuse* 18:3 (2006), 279–88.
5 Sarah Ben-David and Leonard Weller, "Religiosity, Criminality and Types of Offences of Jewish Male Prisoners," *Medicine and Law* 14:7–8 (1995), 509–19.
6 Meredith Blackman, "American Orthodox Women and Domestic Violence: An Intervention Design," *Advocates' Forum*, 2010, ssa.uchicago.edu/american-orthodox-jewish-women-and-domestic-violence-intervention-design.
7 Erzen, *God in Captivity*, 32–33.
8 For instance, before serving time for soliciting sex from a minor (actually a federal agent posing as a minor) online, NARSOL Robin Vander Wall headed the far-right Faith and Family Alliance and was campaign chair for Virginia politician Bob McDonnell, called "Taliban Bob" for his virulent opposition to gay rights, contraception, and abortion, and his campaigns for draconian sex offense penalties. Max Blumenthal, "The Virginia GOP's Dirty Money," *Nation*, November 4, 2005.
9 "Importance of Religion in One's Life," Pew Research Center, n.d., pewforum.org/religious-landscape-study/importance-of-religion-in-ones-life.

## 10 Men Face Masculinity

1 Jesse Fruhwirth, "Male Call: A Conversation about Masculinity and Violence with Byron Hurt and Jackson Katz," *Bitch*, July 24, 2018, bitchmedia.org/article/a-conversation-about-masculinity-and-violence.
2 See "Department of Defense," Mentors in Violence Prevention (MVP) Strategies official website, mvpstrat.com/mvp-programs/department-of-defense.
3 Greg Myre, "Despite Prevention Programs, Sexual Assaults Rise at Military Academies," *NPR*, February 14, 2019, npr.org/2019/02/14/

694597943/despite-prevention-programs-sexual-assaults-rise-at-military-academies.

4 Jim Walsh, "A Call to Men: Stepping Outside the 'Man Box,'" *MinnPost*, August 7, 2017, minnpost.com/arts-culture/2017/08/call-men-stepping-outside-man-box.

5 Alan Greig et al., "Challenging Male Supremacy: Accountability and the Experiences of a New York Collective," Men Engage Alliance, 2016, menengage.blogspot.com/2016/03/challenging-male-supremacy.html.

## 11 Another Women's Movement

1 Roger N. Lancaster, *Sex Panic and the Punitive State* (Berkeley: University of California Press, 2011), 197–8.

2 "Defending the Indefensible? Plea to Clean Sex Offender Registry," KENS5, June 25, 2014, legacy.kens5.com/story/news/local/2014/06/25/10304436.

3 See Women Against Registry official website, womenagainstregistry.org.

4 "Sex Offender Registries and Calls for Reform," *Diane Rehm Show*, July 7, 2015, thedianerehmshow.org/shows/2015-07-07/sex-offender-registries-and-calls-for-reform.

5 Julian Bond, "Self-Defense against Rape: The Joanne Little Case," *Black Scholar* 6:6 (1975), 29–31; Joan Barthel, "Convicting a Battered Woman," *New York Times*, September 25, 1985. See also Emily Thuma, *All Our Trials: Prisons, Policing, and the Feminist Fight to End Violence* (Champaign: University of Illinois Press, 2019).

6 Judith Levine, "A Tale of Two Migrants: Farmworker and Sex Worker," *Seven Days*, July 17, 2013, sevendaysvt.com/vermont/a-tale-of-two-migrants-farmworker-and-sex-worker/Content?oid=2243944.

7 Svati P. Shah, "Trafficking and the Conflation with Sex Work: Implications for HIV Prevention and Control," Working Paper, UN Global Commission for HIV and the Law, 2011.

8 HR 1865, Allow States and Victims to Fight Online Sex Trafficking Act of 2017, 115th Congress (2017–18).

9 Melissa Farley, Kenneth Franzblau, and M. Alexis Kennedy, "Online Prostitution and Trafficking," *Albany Law Review* 77:3 (2014), 1039–94, albanylawreview.org/Articles/Vol77_3/77.3.1039%20Farley%20Franzblau%20Kennedy.pdf.

10 Janet Mackeod et al., "Challenging Men's Demand for Prostitution in Scotland," Women's Support Project, 2008, whiteribbonscotland.files.wordpress.com/2008/04/challenging_mens_demand.pdf.

11 National Council of State Legislatures Human Trafficking Enactment Database, subheads "Sex Trafficking Crimes" and "Trafficking of Children and Youth," 2017, ncsl.org/research/civil-and-criminal-justice/human-trafficking-enactment-database.aspx.

12 Melissa Gira Grant, "FOSTA Backers to Sex Workers: Your Work Can

Never Be Safe," *Appeal,* April 24, 2018, theappeal.org/fosta-backers-to-sex-workers-your-work-can-never-be-safe-5a67582e04f3.

13 Hélène le Bail, Calogero Giametta, and Noemi Rassouw, "What Do Sex Workers Think about the French Prostitution Act?," Médecins du Monde, April 2018, medecinsdumonde.org/en/actualites/publications/2018/04/12/study-impact-law-13-april-2016-against-prostitution-system-france.

14 Laura E. Durso and Gary J. Gates, "Serving Our Youth: LGBT Homeless Youth Provider Survey," UCLA Williams Institute, 2012, williamsinstitute.law.ucla.edu/press/americas-shame-40-of-homeless-youth-are-lgbt-kids.

15 Meredith Dank, Jennifer Yahner, and Kuniko Madden, "Surviving the Streets of New York: Experiences of LGBTQ Youth, YMSM, and YWSW Engaged in Survival Sex," Urban Institute, 2015, urban.org/research/publication/surviving-streets-new-york-experiences-lgbtq-youth-ymsm-and-ywsw-engaged-survival-sex.

16 While YWEP closed in 2013, their reports and other documentation of their organization and political education are available online at youarepriceless.org.

17 Several excellent books have recently been published by sex worker organizer–writers. See, e.g., Melissa Gira Grant, *Playing the Whore: The Work of Sex Work* (New York and London: Verso, 2014); and Juno Mac and Molly Smith, *Revolting Prostitutes: The Fight for Sex Worker Rights* (New York and London: Verso, 2018).

18 Jordon Flaherty, "Her Crime: Sex Work in New Orleans," *Colorlines*, January 13, 2010, colorlines.com/articles/her-crime-sex-work-new-orleans; "Sex Offender Registration for Sex Workers Ends in Louisiana," Louisiana Justice Institute, June 28, 2011, louisianajusticeinstitute.blogspot.com/2011/06/sex-offender-registration-for-sex.html.

## 12 Restorative and Transformative Justice: Making the Road

1 Like the South African Truth and Reconcilliation Commission, the Gacaca courts were not without their limitations and critics. See, e.g., "Rwanda and South Africa: A Long Road from Truth to Reconcilliation, *Conversation*, April 26, 2017, theconversation.com/rwanda-and-south-africa-a-long-road-from-truth-to-reconciliation-75628.

2 "35 States Encourage Restorative Justice as Prison Alternative," *Crime and Justice News*, July 20, 2016, thecrimereport.org/2016/07/20/35-states-encourage-restorative-justice-as-prison-alternative.

3 The Communication Initiative Network, RESTORE, comminit.com/content/responsibility-and-equity-sexual-transgressions-offering-restorative-experience-restore.

4 American Bar Association Criminal Justice Section Task Force on College Due Process Rights and Victim Protections, "Recommendations for Colleges And Universities in Resolving Allegations of Campus Sexual Misconduct," American Bar Association, June 8, 2017, americanbar.org/news/abanews/aba-news-archives/2017/06/aba_task_force_onco.

5 University of Colorado–Boulder Restorative Justice Program, *CURJ Annual Report 2017/18.*

6 Jessica Pishko, "Restorative Justice' for Shoplifting? A Court Calls It Extortion," *The Nation*, October 30, 2017, thenation.com/article/restorative-justice-for-shoplifting-a-court-calls-it-extortion.

7 INCITE! and Critical Resistance, "Statement on Gender Violence and the Prison-Industrial Complex," 2001, incite-national.org/incite-critical-resistance-statement.

8 "Maria Posters the Subways and Confronts Her Family," Community United Against Violence Storytelling and Organizing Project, CUAV, 2009–10, stopviolenceeveryday.org/wp-content/uploads/maria-posters-the-subway.pdf.

9 "Sistas Makin' Moves: Collective Leadership for Personal Transformation and Social Justice / Sista II Sista," in *Color of Violence: The INCITE! Anthology* (Durham: Duke University Press, 2016), 196–207.

10 Zarley, B. David, "For poet and activist Malcolm London, words are no longer enough," *a beautiful perspective*, abeautifulperspective.com/2018/03/poet-activist-malcolm-london-words-no-longer-enough.

11 "Summary Statement Re: Community Accountability Process (March 2017)," Transforming Harm, transformharm.tumblr.com. See also Charlene A. Carruthers, *Unapologetic: A Black, Queer, Feminist Mandate for Radical Movements* (Beacon Press, 2018).

12 See Mia Mingus, "Pods and Pod Mapping Worksheet," Bay Area Transformative Justice Collective, June 2016, batjc.wordpress.com/pods-and-pod-mapping-worksheet.

13 Community United Against Violence, "This Queer Year: Report Back 2009/10," cuav.org/wp-content/uploads/2012/09/summer-2010_web.pdf.

14 Generation Five, *Transformative Justice Handbook*, 2017, generationfive.org/wp-content/uploads/2017/06/Transformative-Justice-Handbook.pdf.

## Reform or Radical Change?

1 Ruth Wilson Gilmore, speech delivered at "The Revolution Will Not Be Funded: Beyond the Nonprofit Industrial Complex," University of California, Santa Barbara, California, 2004.

2 André Gorz, *Strategy for Labor: A Radical Proposal* (Boston: Beacon, 1967). Ruth Wilson Gilmore has expanded and popularized this idea

more recently, particularly in relation to prison-industrial-complex abolition.

## 2. Demedicalize Sexual Violence

1 Dean Spade, "'Having a Cause' versus Living a Life Centered in Radical Transformation," Deanspade.net blog post, November 23, 2018, deanspade.net/tag/mutual-aid.

## 3. Decriminalize Child and Teen Sexuality

1 David T. Evans, *Sexual Citizenship: The Material Construction of Sexualities* (London: Routledge, 1993), 215.

## 5. Complicate Consent

1 Jake New, "The 'Yes Means Yes' World," *Inside Higher Education*, October 17, 2014, insidehighered.com/news/2014/10/17/colleges-across-country-adopting-affirmative-consent-sexual-assault-policies.
2 Zoe D. Peterson and Charlene L. Muehlenhard, "Conceptualizing the 'Wantedness' of Women's Consensual and Nonconsensual Sexual Experiences: Implications for How Women Label Their Experiences with Rape," *Journal of Sex Research* 44:1 (2007), 72–88.

## 6. Eroticize Safety, Proliferate Pleasures

1 adrienne marie brown, "The Return of the Pleasure Activist," November 11, 2010, adriennemareebrown.net/2010/11/11/the-return-of-the-pleasure-activist.
2 Centers for Disease Control and Prevention, "HIV and AIDS—United States, 1981–2000" (Erratum), *MMWR Weekly* 50:47 (November 30, 2001).
3 Douglas Crimp, "Liberation Backlash," *Sex Panic!* (New York, 1997), 12, available at archive.qzap.org/index.php/Detail/Object/Show/object_id/551.
4 Jim Eigo, "The Monogamy Code," *Sex Panic!*, 19.
5 Just Beginnings Collaborative, Justbeginnings.org
6 (Re)Nude* SEX(uality) Coaching, igrivera.com/renude-sexuality-coaching.html.

7 Audre Lorde, "Uses of the Erotic: The Erotic as Power," in *Sister Outsider: Essays and Speeches* (Freedom, CA: Crossing Press, 1984), 53–9.

## 7. Build and Sustain a Robust Welfare State, Not a Carceral State

1 Marie Gottschalk, *Caught: The Prison State and the Lockdown of American Politics* (Princeton and Oxford: Princeton University Press, 2015), 32.
2 Samuel Bowles and Arjun Jayadev, "One Nation Under Guard," *New York Times*, February 15, 2014, opinionator.blogs.nytimes.com/2014/02/15/one-nation-under-guard.
3 World Inequality Index 2018, wir2018.wid.world/executive-summary.html.
4 See Ulrich Beck, *Risk Society: Towards a New Modernity* (Newbury Park: Sage Publications Inc., 1992), as well as Beck's numerous other books on the subject.
5 Frank Newport, "Democrats More Positive about Socialism than Capitalism," *Gallup*, August 13, 2018, news.gallup.com/poll/240725/democrats-positive-socialism-capitalism.aspx.

## 8. Think Intersectionally

1 Audre Lorde, "Learning from the Sixties," address given at Harvard University celebration of Malcolm X, February 1982, blackpast.org/african-american-history/1982-audre-lorde-learning-60s.
2 Cherríe Moraga and Gloria Anzaldúa, eds., *This Bridge Called My Back: Writings by Radical Women of Color* (New York: Kitchen Table / Women of Color Press, 1981).

## 9. Practice Restorative and Transformative Justice

1 "Position Statement of the National Association of Black Social Workers," May 29, 1968, reprinted in National Association of Black Social Workers, *Harambee: Thirty Years of Unity* (conference flier, New Orleans, 1998), cdn.ymaws.com/ nabsw.org/resource/collection/E1582D77-E4CD-4104-996A-D42D08F9CA7D/NABSW_30_Years_of_Unity_-_Our_Roots_Position_Statement_1968.pdf.

## 10. Embrace Abolition Feminism

1 Caitlin Davies, "'Bad Girls' in Holloway Prison: When Being a 'Loud' Black Woman Was an Offence in Itself," *Open Democracy*, August 30, 2018, opendemocracy.net/5050/caitlin-davies/bad-girls-in-holloway-prison-black-women-extract.

2 See Reclaim Holloway, reclaimholloway.strikingly.com/

3 Faye Honey Knopp, "On Radical Feminism and Abolition," *Peace Review: A Journal of Social Justice* 6:2 (1994), 203–8.

4 INCITE! and Critical Resistance, "Statement on Gender Violence and the Prison-Industrial Complex," 2001, incite-national.org/incite-critical-resistance-statement.

5 Angela Y. Davis, "Feminism and Abolition: Theories and Practices for the Twenty-First Century," address given at the University of Chicago, May 2013, youtube.com/watch?v=koieCAUWGnM.

# Index